THE BOOTSY EGAN LETTERS

THE
BOOTSY
EGAN
Letters

COLIN WARD

Best Wishes

Colin Ward

MAINSTREAM
PUBLISHING

EDINBURGH AND LONDON

First published in Great Britain in 1997 by
MAINSTREAM PUBLISHING COMPANY (EDINBURGH) LTD
7 Albany Street
Edinburgh EH1 3UG

ISBN 1 85158 908 2

A catalogue record for this book is available from the British Library

Typeset in Berkeley, Garamond and Gill Sans
Printed and bound in Great Britain by Butler and Tanner Ltd, Frome

'Buy this book or I'll send
the boys round!'

William Egan

Guildford Road
Leatherhead
Surrey KT24 5NW

Graham Kelly
Chief Executive
The Football Association
16 Lancaster Gate
London W2 3LW

11 August 1996

Dear Graham,

No disrespect, Graham, but I did once hear you described as having had a charisma bypass. Not in my book, I might add. You look OK to me. Take some of the credit for the summer of glorious content. Football came home thanks to you. Now is the time to turn this media circus to your advantage, and I am the man to help you.

I've done my time at the sharp end but now, like the rest of football, I've got a new edge. No longer the thug you used to love to hate, I'm now into security for the famous with videos as a sideline – and have I got one for you.

The GK exercise video. A sure-fire image-builder for yourself. No longer the gruff, unsmiling exterior but the FA's Mr Motivator. Your good self with three leotard lovelies (I might have to put you in a slightly baggy England shirt, for obvious reasons. The image I can build, but I can't get rid of the midriff) working out to a succession of overdubbed football songs.

Just imagine: 'We're playing for England, Engerland,' with yourself doing light exercise movements and talking along with the famous GK voice. Fame, fortune and no more snide remarks from the tabloids from now on in.

Now, I've got Max down the Magic Eye studio who owes me, so you just give me the word and I'll get the girls fixed. I'm due at the Marco-Pierre White restaurant Wednesday week with somebody famous, so I could pop in before lunch for a chat and a few girlie portfolios for you to look at. Tell me, do you want slightly tubbier girls?

Your man still singing 'Three Lions',

William Egan

The Football Association Limited
Founded 1863
16 Lancaster Gate, London W2 3LW

Mr W. Egan
Guildford Road
Leatherhead
Surrey KT24 5NW

27 September 1996

Dear Bill,

Thanks for the offer, but I'm back into training for next year's Great North Run – hoping to beat my personal best of 2 hours 5 minutes – so will be unable to take advantage of the leotard lovelies.

Maybe another time?

Yours sincerely,

Graham Kelly
Chief Executive

Guildford Road
Leatherhead
Surrey KT24 5NW

Alex Ferguson
Manager
Manchester United Football Club
Sir Matt Busby Way
Old Trafford
Manchester M16 0RA

26 August 1996

Dear Alex,

As an ex-Terrace Terror of no mean repute (I used to be known as 'Bootsy'), I am writing to you as the custodian of all that looks fierce. It was once said that the blue meanies down the road would brown their pants when I gave them a scowl, but I think that your outbursts have usurped even me – which brings me to the point.

I have a daughter, Georgina, named after the great one (how will today's lot fare with Eric and Ryan?), and I am having a lot of trouble getting her off to sleep at night. I was wondering if you could send me a picture of yourself in full growlism mode. I could then stick it on the wall as a sort of bogeyman. That should stop her getting out of bed at night. It will probably scare the living daylights out of my dog as well, but if it helps me to keep my daughter in bed then it will have been worth it.

Please don't send the one where you are attacking the referee or really spitting blood, as I don't want her to suffer nightmares or problems in later life. I would also appreciate you sending my wife a signed picture of yourself smiling, as she reckons your face would crack if you ever did and I want to prove her wrong.

Your man in the latest away shirt!

Yours sincerely,

SENT SIGNED PHOTOGRAPH

William Egan

9

Guildford Road
Leatherhead
Surrey KT24 5NW

Alex Ferguson
Manager
Manchester United Football Club
Sir Matt Busby Way
Old Trafford
Manchester M16 0RA

9 September 1996

Dear Alex,

I opened my mail this morning to be met with a Manchester United programme and a picture of yourself advertising the museum and trophy room. On the cover you look thoughtful (no doubt wondering how Shearer got away to those flared-trouser Geordies).

Anyway, that picture isn't you and you haven't signed it. Looking at the way the envelope was addressed it might have been done by the tea lad. This isn't the way Manchester United should act.

I appreciate that you are busy planning the assault on the European Cup but my daughter is being particularly troublesome, so how about one where you are really giving it the 'Govan Growl'?

I hereby enclose some change from a trip to Fenerbahce and I look forward to receiving my photograph in due course. This money should come in handy for next year's European campaign, because we always get at least one Turkish delight.

Down with the Geordies!

Here's to European conquest!

Yours sincerely,

William Egan

The Manchester United Football Club plc
Sir Matt Busby Way, Old Trafford, Manchester M16 0RA

Mr W. Egan
Guildford Road
Leatherhead
Surrey KT24 5NW

31 December 1996

Dear Mr Egan,

Thank you for your letter dated 9 September and please forgive the delay in replying.

I have noted your comments, but am not sure which photographs you refer to.

I am returning your Turkish money herewith and I would like to take this opportunity of thanking you for your loyal support.

Yours sincerely,

Alex Ferguson CBE
Manager

Guildford Road
Leatherhead
Surrey KT24 5NW

Bill Buford
Editor, The New Yorker
20 West 43rd Street
New York
NY 10036-7441

26 August 1996

Dear Bill,

Remember that book you wrote a few years ago called *Among the Thugs*? 'Well-written tripe' was how one thug described it. However, thinking you were one of us I enrolled on an English literature correspondence course. Based upon my newly discovered literary talent, I believe you might be interested in a new angle for your magazine aimed at the discerning American reader.

Being an editor, and as such under more pressure than Gaddafi's diplomatic corps, you need real stories of bite and substance. This story told by myself will inform your readers about the way the press act with regard to sport in the UK, which I believe is different from that in the US, where sportswriters are a revered bunch of chaps.

As we all know, football came home to England in the summer and the hooligans all stayed at home. Or did they? I believe that they are alive and well and inhabiting the press box. That's the story. Instead of the press writing about the hooligans, how about a hooligan writing about the press? I reckon that story would go down a storm in the US, where all things British are news.

Let me introduce myself. I am William 'Bootsy' Egan, ex-Chelsea Shed football hooligan of some repute. Writer turned fighter who has just earned my first GCSE in English literature. I believe I can write the true story about how these highly paid scribes vilify our football manager, who should be a treasured institution instead of a hack's whipping post, in a way which will entertain and enlighten.

But don't just take my word for it. How about this for poignant prose? The scene is the press box at England's national stadium during the recent

European Football Championships. Harry Harris (Daily Mirror tabloid writer) is talking to Hugh McIlvanney (Observer broadsheet heavyweight):

'Hugh, you're a stupid jock twit who is jealous of English football.'

'Maybe so, but at least I'm not an ugly big-nosed git who hates the England *soccer* manager Terry Venables and gets lampooned by his own editor.'

The Daily Mirror ran a story putting Harry Harris in the stocks as punishment for doubting England's football ability when it became apparent that England had a chance after all. The italics are to explain to yourself as an American who Terry Venables is. You know: one people separated by a common language.

Stuff like that will wow your readers as well as give an insight into the cosy, bigoted world in which the UK sportswriting cognoscenti operate. Now that Godly Glenn is in charge I am sure that the story will really take off, appealing to the God-fearing side of America. I can see the Sun headline now when it all goes wrong again: FOR GOD'S SAKE . . .

I await your reply on this matter, as well as details on accreditation and payment terms.

Yours sincerely,

William Egan

English version copies sent to: The Sunday Times
                                  The People
                                  The Guardian

The New Yorker
20 West 43rd Street, New York, NY 10036-7441

William Egan
Guildford Road
Leatherhead
Surrey KT24 5NW

9 September 1996

Dear Bill,

Thank you for your amusing letter, which I enjoyed. I like your idea – and the limited time I spent with the British sports journalists proved to me that your thesis (that *they're* the hooligans) is absolutely true. But I don't think it's a story for an American magazine.

Good luck with the writing.

Yours sincerely,

Bill Buford

The Sunday Times
1 Pennington Street, London E1 9XW

Mr W. Egan
Guildford Road
Leatherhead
Surrey KT24 5NW

4 September 1996

Dear Mr Egan,

Thank you for your letter and your idea of a 'poacher-turned-gamekeeper' piece. I don't think it's one for us, however, but wish you luck placing it elsewhere.

Yours sincerely,

Jeff Randall
Sports Editor

The People
Sunday Newspaper of the Year – National Newspaper of the Year

William Egan Esq.
Guildford Road
Leatherhead
Surrey KT24 5NW

4 September 1996

Dear Bill,

I don't know about Gaddafi's diplomatic corps but you were right. A vast number of letters I receive are forgotten by the tea break – but yours is an exception.

I don't know whether we could use your ideas, but how would you like to come into the office one day and we could have a chat about this and that?

If you fancy a cup of tea or maybe even a pint of something stronger, give me a ring on a Tuesday or a Wednesday.

Yours sincerely,

Ed Barry
Sports Editor

The Guardian
Weekend Magazine
119 Farringdon Road, London EC1R 3ER

William Egan
Guildford Road
Leatherhead
Surrey KT24 5NW

9 September 1996

Dear William Egan,

Thanks for your letter. Your idea sounds very interesting but I'm afraid that since I don't know your writing I can't offer you a firm commission. However, if you'd like to submit a piece of around 3,500 words on spec, I'll be happy to consider it for publication. Thanks again.

Yours sincerely,

Deborah Orr
Editor, Guardian Weekend

Guildford Road
Leatherhead
Surrey KT24 5NW

Deborah Orr
Editor
Guardian Weekend Magazine
119 Farringdon Street
London EC1R 3ER

11 September 1996

Dear Ms Orr,

I must assume you are a Ms because everybody who is female and making it big in newspapers is a Ms.

Anyway, 'on spec'! You're having a laugh. How does one do an inside piece on the press on spec? Read the back pages then make it up. Come to think of it, that's what the tabloids do, so why not? However, I approached your mob because you're the voice of truth and the people want to read the truth about the press boys who write all that horrid stuff about our national heroes. Arise Sir Terry Venables and your Reverence Glenn.

Still, one GCSE isn't really a CV but that doesn't matter. Who is the top notcher in the writing stakes? Clive James: Fat, bald Aussie with a large Tarbie. So I will take you up on your offer. You get me press accreditation for the away match in Poland and I'll give you an on-spec spectacular with superior specifications, and I promise I won't nut any of those time-wasting liars.

The ball is in your half of the field, but don't pick it up and run. We're talking round ball game here.

Your man with the thesaurus,

William Egan

The Guardian
Weekend Magazine
119 Farringdon Road, London EC1R 3ER

William Egan
Guildford Road
Leatherhead
Surrey KT24 5NW

18 September 1996

Dear William Egan,

Thanks for your letter. I'm afraid, however, that I didn't understand it.
Sorry and thanks again.

Yours sincerely,

Deborah Orr
Editor, Guardian Weekend

Guildford Road
Leatherhead
Surrey KT24 5NW

Glenn Hoddle
England Manager
The Football Association
16 Lancaster Gate
London W2 3LW

26 August 1996

Dear Glenn,

Congratulations on your appointment as England manager. It doesn't matter that you weren't first choice and the old FA dodderers at Lancaster Gate asked the world and his dog before they got to your door; the main thing is a man who once worked under someone called Arsenal is now in charge.

However, there are a couple of points bothering me. I understand that you have discovered God. Did you discover him running down the wing at Spurs when a crazed full-back was coming at you with malice? Or perhaps you received an almighty rollicking from the missus when you slipped away for a crafty bet on the tables when you were based in Monaco, used God as a way out, and haven't yet had the heart to tell her indoors the truth?

You see, as an avid England fan, I am worried that if your allegiance to the almighty is not cast iron, then the first game England lose will see yourself on the back pages: IN THE NAME OF GOD GO, or PRAY FOR ENGLAND NOW. Imagine the upset if the faith isn't solid.

I am also worried about your choice of assistant. John Gorman looks like a Greek waiter who serves you a dodgy kebab late on a Saturday after a good home win, or, worse still, one of those San Francisco types. I hope you can vouch for him. It must be remembered that the success of recent years has been founded on the Don Howe/Arsenal connection.

Notwithstanding these worries, I wonder if you could send my wife a picture of yourself as she thinks you are quite dishy, but without Mr Tache, if you please.

I look forward to hearing from you.

Yours sincerely,

NO REPLY

William Egan

Guildford Road
Leatherhead
Surrey KT24 5NW

David Dein
Vice Chairman
Arsenal Football Club
Arsenal Stadium
Highbury
London N5 1BU

26 August 1996

Dear David,

Once again you seem to be getting worse press than Hannibal Lector. Is it because you always seem so groomed that you could be a bit-part actor on *Dynasty* without the Grecian 2000, or is there something else? Still, as a dyed-in-the-wool Northbanker of years past, it doesn't matter to me whether or not you were right or wrong to sack Bruce Rioch, the main thing is the team.

Quite how you managed not to sign one of the 20 players Bruce gave you when you were instrumental in setting up the new transfer system after George took the dodgy florins is beyond me, but that is for the tabloids to sort out when they hear Bruce's side.

I don't know about yourself but I am sick and tired of Arsenal being the butt of everybody's jokes, so I am writing to offer you the services of the Northbank protection team. At the next shareholders' meeting we will duff up anybody who doubts your word. From what I have heard about the last one you had a few plants in the audience who stood up to state how you were on the mobile throughout the European Championships, trying to sign players.

Forget that. Just call in myself and a few of the lads who made their name in the real world. 'Insult Dein and you insult Arsenal. Take that, you spotty tabloid plant.' With that we can dish the nut and help them down the stairs head first.

Our credentials are impeccable. Strace the Ace has done a ten for wounding with intent, Crusher Chits did a five for an attack on a rival pub and Frenchy has two 'not guiltys' at the Bailey. Ask the wrong questions in front of that lot at your peril, mate, eh?

I await your reply on this matter.

Yours sincerely,

William Egan

NO REPLY

20

Guildford Road
Leatherhead
Surrey KT24 5NW

Francis Lee
Chairman
Manchester City Football Club
Maine Road
Manchester M14 7WN

26 August 1996

Dear Francis,

I think I have discovered the route to success for Manchester City. Even though my allegiance is with the Arsenal I wish to see the red Man U monster curbed and the only way to do this is the re-emergence of a strong City.

I now realise that the previous chairman, Peter Swales, was suffering from a massive inferiority complex and would only appoint men for the job whom he felt were not going to get more publicity than he was. His plans for City were always obscured by his own Freudian failings. I now feel that you are perhaps suffering from the curse of Swales in so much as you might have a height complex. You probably don't realise you have inherited this curse, but how else can you explain the dismal run of results? The curse might explain why you have appointed Alan Ball as manager. I believe this man is actually shorter than yourself.

Mind you, that didn't stop you in your heyday. I have seen the slap you gave Norman 'bites yer legs' Hunter in front of 45,000 in the old *Match of the Day* footage and he was all of 5ft 9ins tall. So you see that I am not mocking your lack of inches, rather implying that your determination to show people that a lack of inches doesn't mean lack of inspiration or will to win may be clouding your judgement.

There is no doubt in my mind that Bally will not survive the curse of Christmas, so I look to see you appointing someone over 5ft 6ins tall to exorcise the curse of Swales and push the blues forward to their rightful place on the podium.

I await your reply on this matter.

Yours sincerely,

NO REPLY

William Egan

Guildford Road
Leatherhead
Surrey KT24 5NW

Ken Bates
Chairman
Chelsea Football Club
Stamford Bridge
London SW6 1HS

10 September 1996

Dear Ken,

What is the fat boy Matthew Harding up to? He dares call himself a blues man and an ex-Shed boy, then gives money to the reds. You didn't save Chelsea FC to have pinko labour poofters enter the Bridge, did you? Too much money as a kid, I reckon.

If he wants to support the reds, then let him go and support that bunch of duffers the other side of the water. No wonder they came back from a 2–0 deficit the other night; they got their inspiration from looking at that commie red lover.

Boot him out forthwith. Better still, let me and a few of the boys come up in the royal box and dangle him over the parapet in front of John and Dave 'The Gap' Mellor.

Come on you blues.

Support John Major.

Your man in blue,

William Egan

Chelsea Football Club
Stamford Bridge, London SW6 1HS

Mr W. Egan
Guildford Road
Leatherhead
Surrey KT24 5NW

17 September 1996

Dear Bill,

Thank you for your letter dated 10 September 1996, but if you wish to make comments like that I suggest you direct them to Matthew Harding himself.

Yours sincerely,

Ken Bates
Chairman

Guildford Road
Leatherhead
Surrey KT24 5NW

HRH The Prince of Wales
c/o Buckingham Palace
London SW1

10 September 1996

Your Royal Highness,

Fact of the matter, Charlie, is that you are about as popular as a BSE beefburger. Why, I ask myself? Poor PR? Try as you might, you are barking up the wrong tree. Who's advising you? Those Oxbridge types, that's who. What you need is some sound advice so the masses will love you once more.

Look at us lot. Crusher Chits, Strace the Ace, Mad Monty and myself used to be about as welcome as Terry Venables at Alan Sugar's birthday party, so much so that whole armies of police were employed following us around. Now look at us: more popular than your ex-missus.

There's the rub. Turn this love of all things football to suit yourself. Get yourself pictured in a football shirt, be seen kicking a ball with the lads. Forget horses; they are OK in the private life, but to become King and a man of the people you've got to ooze footy appeal.

Mandela understands. From heinous terrorist to preferred palm presser in one snap shot. Every photo shoot he's there, kicking a ball. Your man with the tan Juan Carlos, King of Spain. When the ball hit the onion bag in the football final of the Olympics, he was up there dancing with the best of them. Do you think he would have missed the chance to be seen singing 'Three Lions' this summer? Not a chance. Sorry, mate, you blew it big time.

What you need is a trip to the match where the real lads hang out. We are available for photo shoots at reasonable rates and we are often in the Buck Palace area doing security, should you and the bear heads fancy a kick around.

Boot the equine erks (little naval slang there) into touch. Get with the real men and liven up your image.

Yours sincerely,

William Egan

St James's Palace
London SW1A 1BS

1 November 1996

Dear Mr Egan,

Thank you for your letter addressed to The Prince of Wales. I am sure you will understand that His Royal Highness receives many letters each day and is unable to reply personally to them all. Nevertheless, His Royal Highness is grateful to you for writing and has asked me to send you his best wishes.

Yours sincerely,

Clair Southwell

Guildford Road
Leatherhead
Surrey KT24 5NW

Steve Coppell
Manager
Manchester City Football Club
Maine Road
Manchester M14 7WN

26 October 1996

Dear Steve,

I recently wrote to Franny Lee about his next manager. However, I did not realise that my letter would initiate the sacking of Mr Alan 'Squeaky Voice' Ball.

However, I did point out to Franny that when Bally left (I predicted Christmas) it would be bad form to try and employ somebody who was shorter than himself. Please can you confirm that you are taller than Franny, because if you are not I would not cancel your subscription to *Marketing* magazine as you may need the inside back pages (job ads) very shortly.

Just one question to yourself: Have you employed Phil Neal? Is he the same person we saw on TV with Graham Taylor on the infamous documentary when his sole contribution was to chant back Turnip Head's comments? Remember the Poland match: 'Get Wrighty on, eh?' 'Yes, boss, Wrighty on, Wrighty on.'

I cannot believe that you will operate the same regime with your academic background. I would assume that you are looking for a more reasoned, studious and reflective arena to bounce ideas around.

Let's get back to the big time.

Blue is the colour.

William Egan

Manchester City plc
Maine Road, Moss Side, Manchester M14 7WN

Dear Mr Egan,

This was the reply given to me by Steve Coppell to your letter. Unfortunately he was unable to sign it before he left.

Manager's Secretary

Mr William Egan
Guildford Road
Leatherhead
Surrey KT24 5NW

5 November 1996

Dear Mr Egan,

Thank you very much for your letter and good wishes.

I just hope I can repay the faith that has been placed in me by Francis Lee and the Manchester City supporters.

I must admit that at the present time every City supporter I meet has a different solution to our problems, and it is my responsibility to seek answers to the present woes.

I hope I am given the time and patience to achieve this considerable goal.

Once again, thank you for writing.

Yours sincerely,

Steve Coppell
Manager

Guildford Road
Leatherhead
Surrey KT24 5NW

Graeme Souness
Manager
Southampton Football Club
The Dell
Milton Road
Southampton SO15 2XH

28 October 1996

Dear Graeme,

Magic, mate. You stuffed those overpaid reds from Manchester. What a tonking! Six goals to three!

Out they came like growling tigers, but by the time it was over they were limping back to Manchester with 'The Saints Go Marching In' ringing in their ears. They couldn't even find an excuse, like changing their shirts at half-time! It was like the days when you used to take no prisoners.

Just where did you find those two foreign unpronounceables? Who cares, though, when they can break the onion bag like that.

Anyway, I've decided to send you some of my foreign money towards the next foreigner you are going to buy. I've included a shekel because there must be more where Berkovitch came from.

I include a Southampton joke for you to tell the new foreign lads to make them feel more at home.

Knock Knock.
Who's there?
Owen.
Owen who?
Owen the Saints Go Marching In.

Yours sincerely,

William Egan

SENT SIGNED PHOTOGRAPH

Enc. 1 Israeli shekel

28

Guildford Road
Leatherhead
Surrey KT24 5NW

Private and Confidential

Bobby Robson
Manager
Barcelona Football Club
Barcelona
Spain

28 October 1996

Dear Bobby,

My friends and I have been faithfully following England for a number of years now and we met you in Stockholm, although the sight of my mate Ginger Ward in his brown leather coat did cause you some discomfort, as you thought he was a crazed stalker.

Well, me and the lads have come up with a wheeze to get back at the sportswriting fraternity. We thought that we would present a trophy to the sportswriter who had excelled above and beyond the call of vitriolic abuse in his rubbishing of England managers.

I am just writing to see if you have any nominations for this position. We intend to present the recipient of this award a bottle of foreign beer at the next big England away match. Chits wants to pass it through his kidneys first and smash the empty bottle on his head, but the rest of us feel that this is a little extreme.

Anyway, if you have any nominations we would be pleased to hear from you. If you have any witty ideas for the name of the prize, they would also be gratefully accepted.

Another San Miguel *por favor*,

William Egan, Crusher Chits, Strace the Ace, Frenchy, Ginger Ward

Nomination requests to: Graham Taylor
Terry Venables
Glenn Hoddle
Lawrie McMenemy

FC Barcelona
Av aristides Maillol, s/n 08028 Barcelona

14 November 1996

Hi you guys,

I did receive your letter and appreciate very much your sentiments and disgust at the vitriolic abuse by certain 'sportswriters'?? against England football managers.

The third paragraph of your letter delighted me but I personally do not waste my valuable time and energy in admonishing them. They really are not worth it, and are beyond contempt.

I shall leave it to you as to your reply. The tone of your letter suggested to me that you will not have much trouble in replying in the taste which some of them deserve.

Thank you for taking up the 'baton' on my behalf, and also for your support after so many years.

Pass the Port!

Yours sincerely,

B. Robson

Watford
Registered Office and Ground: Watford Association Football Club Ltd
Vicarage Road Stadium, Watford WD1 8ER

Mr W. Egan
Guildford Road
Leatherhead
Surrey KT24 5NW

1 November 1996

Dear Bill,

I think you are managing quite well without nominations from myself!

Best wishes,

Graham Taylor

From the private office of Terry Venables
213 Putney Bridge Road, London SW15 2NY

Mr W. Egan
Guildford Road
Leatherhead
Surrey KT24 5NW

November 1996

Dear Mr Egan,

Thank you for your recent letter of support. It was kind of you to take time
and trouble to write to me and I do appreciate it.

With all good wishes for Christmas and the New Year,

Terry Venables

Guildford Road
Leatherhead
Surrey KT24 5NW

Jeff Powell
Chief Sportswriter
The Daily Mail
Northcliffe House
2 Derry Street
Kensington
London W8 5TT

28 October 1996

Dear Jeff,

After every England match the lads (Crusher Chits, Mad Monty, Strace the Ace, Frenchy) and I have a chinwag about the worst reportage. Do you guys watch the same match as us? Have any of you ever played football? Anyway, we have decided to award the writer who has shown exceptional 'Diarrhoea d'Ecrire' the order of the beer bottle, or the Turnerip Prize. (A parody of turnip and Turner prize. You can crack that quip in the press box on Saturday, if you like.)

So, Jeff, you have been chosen alongside big-nosed Harry Harris of the Mirror for acrimonious services above and beyond the call of normal sportswriter vitriol. We would like to present you with a bottle of foreign lager, and intend to do so at the next big England away match. Chits wants to pass it through his kidneys first and smash the empty bottle on your head – 'I name this traitor Powell' – but the rest of us feel that this is a little extreme.

You will be pleased to know that this award is only open to bona fide Englishmen – we discount stupid xenophobic jocks (Hugh McIlvanney) and midget micks (John Giles) – so you really are the honoured one.

Anyway, if you have any preferences regarding this then please let us know. I have no doubt you will want to make this into a big media event.

William Egan

NO REPLY

Guildford Road
Leatherhead
Surrey KT24 5NW

Gary Lineker
Football Focus
Television Centre
White City
London

28 October 1996

Dear Gary,

You're the man! Straight out of the shower and really socking it to 'em. What more can a man say?

If only more BBC football presenters realised that you can still be one of the lads and present football as if you were still wearing the white shirt on the Wembley turf, sticking it up those horrible foreigners.

Here's a humorous song for your next appearance.

One Tony Adams
Have only one, Tony Adams, etc.

Yours from a fellow striking python!

William Egan

Gary Lineker

Mr W. Egan
Guildford Road
Leatherhead
Surrey KT24 5NW

6 November 1996

Dear Mr Egan,

Thank you for your letter of 28 October and kind words. They are much appreciated.

Yours sincerely,

Gary Lineker

Guildford Road
Leatherhead
Surrey KT24 5NW

Colin Downey
Referees' Secretary
The Football Association
16 Lancaster Gate
London W2 3LW

28 October 1996

Dear Colin,

I just thought I would offer you a word of advice regarding the amount of flak referees are receiving from the media at the present time, plus an offer of help to tone down some of the criticism.

I have done my fair share of abusing refs and I have to admit that my illustrious colleague Strace the Ace did run on the pitch at Millwall once and try and rearrange the ref's looks, but that is all in the past now.

Mindless violence is behind us (except for when Scotland next play England). We are now in the security business. We have also diversified into other businesses, one of which is temporary tattoos. We all know how tough tattoos make people look, so I was wondering if you would like a special set made up for your Premiership referees? I could even custom-make them for big matches. For example, I could do a special 'Alex Ferguson sucks' with a picture of him sucking a stick of Liverpool rock, or a Vinnie Jones one with a W above an anchor. Imagine that, or a top referee like the much-vilified Paul Danson with a naked lady holding up a red card. Sky cameras would zoom in and this would show the referees up as one of the lads with a sense of humour. The tattoos needn't be permanent.

I can get your custom designs made up within ten days, but I will need a minimum order value of £250 to make it worth my while.

Let's get some respect back for the poor old ref.

William Egan

The Football Association Limited
Founded 1863
16 Lancaster Gate, London W2 3LW

Mr W. Egan
Guildford Road
Leatherhead
Surrey KT24 5NW

1 November 1996

Dear Bill,

Thank you for your letter of 28 October 1996, and how good to hear from you!

Thanks also for the offer of 'visual aid' assistance for Premier League referees. The initial cost of £250, however, does put us off rather – you will appreciate the Football Association's financial position as far as referees are concerned. Little money is available because the players (of course!) are in desperate need of high wages.

Perhaps your own wealthy County Association might be interested? A few Referee Boards of Appeal would provide the additional revenue which might be used to support your latest venture.

Trust all is well for you in the peaceful Surrey countryside.

With best wishes to you and those at Highbury.

Yours sincerely,

Colin Downey
Referees' Secretary

Guildford Road
Leatherhead
Surrey KT24 5NW

Sir Paul Condon
Metropolitan Police Commissioner
New Scotland Yard
London SW1H 0BG

28 October 1996

Dear Sir Paul,

Football came home in the summer thanks to the boys in blue. Showing the
boys in blue giving those dinosaur hoolies the old one-two was terrific TV. It
just goes to prove that you had it taped all along.

However, there was one point which I would like to raise. During one scene
the top-man inspector stopped some Palace half-wit outside a pub. He said
that he had his eye on him and he would check up whether he had paid his
taxes or not if he saw him misbehaving.

Do I deduce from this that the Met now have access to hooligan tax records?
Well, if you have could you please check up on Crusher Chits for me, as he
owes me three William Shakespeares, but he says he is still paying the taxman.
Yet every other Saturday when I see him in the Imperial he is buying some
Doris a beer.

I am prepared to pay the standard fee for this search. I understand that it is
£10 for a run through the hooligan file. I assume that a tax search will be
slightly more.

Hurrah to the end of mindless thuggery!

William Egan

Guildford Road
Leatherhead
Surrey KT24 5NW

Sir Paul Condon
Metropolitan Police Commissioner
New Scotland Yard
London SW1H 0BG

18 January 1997

Dear Sir Paul,

I have received no reply to my letter dated 28 October 1996. I can see that I am missing the point about the way the Metropolitan Police operate.

I therefore enclose £5 towards helping further my request. Is this enough to do a check on Mr John Gorman, assistant manager of the England football team? I am a little bit worried about his character because of the moustache. I am not sure we should be trusting this man to take us into the finals of the World Cup in France.

If there is enough in the pot then perhaps you could do a check on Arsène Wenger, as there are one or two rumours floating around about this man.

I await your reply to my original letter.

Ex-bogeyman turned good guy,

William Egan

Enc. An old £5 note but still legal tender

Metropolitan Police
Sir Paul Condon QPM, Commissioner of Police of the Metropolis
New Scotland Yard, Broadway, London SW1H 0BG

Mr William Egan
Guildford Road
Leatherhead
Surrey KT24 5NW

4 February 1997

Dear Mr Egan,

Thank you for your letter dated 18 January 1997 addressed to the Commissioner asking for a check to be carried out on the assistant manager of the England football team, John Gorman, and enclosing a £5 note to facilitate this request.

I regret that it is not possible to action your request and I am therefore returning your £5 note.

Yours sincerely,

David Jones
Private Secretary to Commissioner

Guildford Road
Leatherhead
Surrey KT24 5NW

Glenn Hoddle
England Manager
The Football Association
16 Lancaster Gate
London W2 3LW

18 January 1997

Dear Glenn,

The looming crunch with the Eyeties grows ever closer. I understand that you favour the pasta diet as promoted by Arsène Wenger.

I hope that with the boys needing to be fired up for the February 'big one' that the pasta diet will be dropped in favour of something more English and substantial.

I propose that we get the lads on the baked potato diet. This is English and makes guys like Dennis Wise feel more at home. Somehow, I don't think many of the lads are cosmopolitan enough to cope with pasta, and we also don't want them to think that anything Italian is superior. We're talking psychology here, something Cloughie, Shanks and Jock Stein were famous for.

I have it on good authority that Fergie stopped the Man U confectionery outlets from selling Turkish delight after their Galatasaray débâcle. Me and the lads are into that positive thinking stuff. After Arsenal lost to Stoke the other season I smashed all the plates. When we lost to Sheffield Wednesday I threw all my cutlery out of the window.

Get the boys in an anti-Italian mood and ban pasta. It's easy for the Polish game; just tell them that cabbage is out.

I await your reply to my original letter and a signed photograph for the wife, which should make up for the fact that sometimes we eat off paper plates with plastic cutlery.

I look forward to hearing from you.
Is God better than Alan Shearer?
England are the best!
See you in Poland!

NO REPLY

William 'Bootsy' Egan

Guildford Road
Leatherhead
Surrey KT24 5NW

John Major
Prime Minister
The House of Commons
London SW1A 0AA

28 January 1997

Dear Fellow Chelsea Fan,

Where were you? There were Chelsea stuffing the Liverpool reds out of sight, and the cameras flashed up on to the balcony, but there was no picture of a beaming Chelsea man. How could you miss the significance of this the day before you meet the election team for a pep talk? The blues wiped the floor with the reds after coming from a seemingly insurmountable deficit, and you weren't there to get the credit.

I'm not an educated man but the people who are advising you are missing the point. I don't know who your spin doctor is, but I doubt whether he could turn a ball enough to bowl out England's middle-order batsmen. Well, he probably could do that as even my aunt Betsy or Two Fingers Flitcroft the gormless butcher could do that. Anyway, enough of that.

You probably missed the best chance to gain popularity you'll ever get. Not only that, but you appeared on the news the next day without your Chelsea jumper on. Don't you realise that Harold Wilson lost an election the night Gerd Muller slipped the third goal past a fumbling Peter Bonetti in 1970?

If the blues beat Leicester and get the Stretford Man U red mob, don't miss it. You'll never get a better chance to be seen to bash the reds again.

The Shed will live.

Ex-Boys Brigade cadet and proud,

William Egan

10 Downing Street
London SW1A 0AA

From the Correspondence Secretary

Mr W. Egan
Guildford Road
Leatherhead
KT24 5NW

31 January 1997

Dear Mr Egan,

The Prime Minister has asked me to thank you for your recent letter.

Yours sincerely,

Frances Slee (Mrs)

Guildford Road
Leatherhead
Surrey KT24 5NW

Mrs Frances S. Lee
Correspondence Secretary
10 Downing Street
London SW1A 0AA

22 March 1997

Dear Mrs Lee,

I recently wrote to John Major with some sound electoral advice about being seen watching football, which I now see he is taking on board.

Imagine my surprise when I received a letter from yourself and I saw that you were named Frances Lee. Are you by any chance related to the pocket-battleship chairman of Manchester City, none other than Francis Lee the First? Or are you such a big fan of the little big man that you have changed your name to impersonate him?

This matter is very important as I have recently received some sound advice from Mr Lee regarding the impartation of a nasty streak into my son, who suffers from the same lack of inches which didn't once affect the upward spiral of Francis.

Come back to me on this one at your earliest convenience.

Yours sincerely,

William Egan

10 Downing Street
London SW1A 2AA

From the Correspondence Secretary

Mr W. Egan
Guildford Road
Leatherhead
KT24 5NW

8 April 1997

Dear Mr Egan,

Thank you for your letter of 22 March. I can tell you that although a football fan myself, I am in no way related to Francis LEE. Unfortunately it would appear that you have misread my surname as Lee instead of Slee.

Yours sincerely,

Francis Slee (Mrs)

Guildford Road
Leatherhead
Surrey KT24 5NW

Howard Wilkinson
Technical Director, English Football
The Football Association
16 Lancaster Gate
London W2 3LW

1 February 1997

Dear Howard,

Congratulations on your new appointment. I look forward to seeing a return to the basics of Anglo-Saxon football as epitomised by your Leeds teams. Correct me if I'm wrong, but I think that you can't beat football played the English way. Get the ball, control it, then pass to another player with the same colour shirt on.

This is the way our Sunday team plays (OK, so Crusher Chits is partial to the odd chest-high tackle and off-the-ball rabbit punch, but we are converting him gradually), and we are successful in the lower reaches of the Leatherhead Sunday League.

What I am writing to you about is the POMO position (Position of Maximum Opportunity). Charles Hughes started it, but despite looking for it on the pitch (as well as in the Kama Sutra), I can't find it.

Is it dead and buried along with the long ball nonsense? If it isn't, could you please explain what it is? I tried to explain a free-kick routine at training the other night and the phrase 'POMO' came up. Someone remarked that I would never make a coach as long as I didn't understand POMO.

Please help me, as in the absence of a reasoned argument I chinned the player.

Your man with the coaching manual,

William 'Coach' Egan

The Football Association Limited
Founded 1863
16 Lancaster Gate, London W2 3LW

Mr William Egan
Guildford Road
Leatherhead
Surrey KT24 5NW

7 February 1997

Dear Bill,

This is just a brief note to thank you for your letter of congratulations dated 1 February.

So far as I understand, the POMO position can best be explained as the position of maximum opportunity in relation to scoring goals. Charles Hughes's theories are contained in a book entitled *The Winning Formula*.

I should emphasise that the 'long ball' is a cliché which has developed over the years, but which has no real meaning in coaching theory.

I do hope this response is helpful to you.

Yours sincerely,

Howard Wilkinson
Technical Director

Guildford Road
Leatherhead
Surrey KT24 5NW

Glenn Hoddle
England Football Manager
The Football Association
16 Lancaster Gate
London W2 3LW

1 February 1997

Dear Glenn,

I have received no reply to my previous requests for a photograph. I have therefore decided to send you some Swiss money which I have left over from one of my previous trips following England when they were managed by your predecessors. I have no doubt that you will be able to bank it as I expect you had a Swiss numbered account when you were playing the tables during your days at Monaco.

Further to my letter dated 18 January I was appalled to switch on the news and see you with a pizza in your face. Didn't you take in any of that stuff about the psychology of forsaking all things Italian? Do you think that the Italian trio at your old Chelsea stomping ground didn't get straight on the blower back to Eyetiesville and tell them that they had seen you eating pizza?

The watchword is all things English. There's time to finish this steak and kidney pie and then go out and beat the Italians. It's all about thinking Anglo-Saxon.

There is a space on my wife's kitchen wall awaiting a photo of your good self. If it helps I will accept one of you with Mr Gorman.

See you at Wembley!

Arrivederci Italia!

France here we come!

KEPT MONEY, SENT SIGNED PHOTOGRAPH

William 'Bootsy' Egan

Enc: 10 Swiss francs

Guildford Road
Leatherhead
Surrey KT24 5NW

Brian Mawhinney
Chairman
The Conservative Party
The House of Commons
London SW1A 0AA

1 February 1997

Dear Brian,

What are you up to? You've got an election to win and on the day the blues came from a huge deficit to stuff the reds 4–2 at Stamford Bridge (even you can recognise the significance of this), Johnny was not there on the balcony to catch the plaudits.

Imagine the publicity this would have created and the inference that would have been taken by the commentators. Elections aren't won by fancy strategy meetings at Chequers, they are won because the masses perceive that the man at the helm can turn things around.

There is even the chance to be seen as pro-European at the same time. You can talk all day about ECUs and such like, but one photo of John shaking hands with Ruud Gullit and the man is seen as understanding Europe.

Harold Wilson recognised that he had lost an election the night West Germany beat England 3–2 in that fateful night in Mexico. You can't afford to miss another chance to get a free burst of publicity. If you do, then it's curtains for you, mate.

Sort your spin doctors out, cos they're bowling on a flat track at the moment and that was your chance to scuff the ball up a bit.

William 'Bootsy' Egan

Guildford Road
Leatherhead
Surrey KT24 5NW

Brian Mawhinney
Chairman
The Conservative Party
The House of Commons
London SW1A 0AA

24 February 1997

Dear Brian,

I have received no reply to my letter of 1 February. What is going on at
Conservative Central Office? Whilst the Kings Road blues go from strength
to strength, Johnny Boy struggles from crisis to crisis.

In his speeches I haven't heard one reference to the blues' (Chelsea's) revival.
He even talks about Europe and doesn't mention Ruud Gullit (Europe and
the black vote). OK, so he might take a little reefer, being Dutch, but did you
hear what he said? 'When someone calls me black I don't get upset, because I
am black.' If you can't score off that statement then visit a brothel!

Do you want me to moonlight and write you a few speeches? I am available
early afternoons if you want me to pop along for a meeting. My fees are
reasonable and I have a diploma in creative writing.

. . . while Labour concentrates solely on defence and holding the line, the
Conservatives are flying along the wing. Suddenly the blue machine cuts in
towards goal and the reds score an own goal.

Come on you blues.

John Major is a 'Shed boy'.

William 'Bootsy' Egan

Conservative Central Office
32 Smith Square, Westminster, London SW1P 3HH

Mr William Egan
Guildford Road
Leatherhead
Surrey KT24 5NW

6 March 1997

Dear Mr Egan,

The party chairman has asked me to thank you for your letters to him of 1 February and 24 February, with sincerest apologies for the delay in response.

We appreciated hearing from you, and thank you for taking the time to write and share your views and suggestions with us in regard to the presentation of Conservative Party policies and our media campaign.

Please be assured that your comments and ideas have been read with interest, and will be brought to the attention of our policy unit.

With all our best wishes to you,

N. Morgan (Mrs)
Public Correspondence

Guildford Road
Leatherhead
Surrey KT24 5NW

Matthew Evans
Chairman
Faber and Faber Ltd
3 Queens Square
London WC1N 3AU

1 February 1997

Dear Mr Evans,

The one thing I learnt in the slammer is that you should always seek out the head honcho, and that is why I am writing to you. As if you didn't know it football is big business nowadays, so please excuse me if I am stating the obvious. Remember the judge who asked: 'Who is Gazza?' Well, I can tell from your office address that you aren't an ostrich, so how about this for a winner?

Hooligan's Rough Guide to Europe

Written by the roughest, toughest hombre ever to drink and fall over in a foreign field. That's me, although I'm now armed with a GCSE in English literature and a correspondence course diploma in creative writing thanks to HM Prison, Maidstone. But I don't need to make this up, because it's all true.

It's all there: drama, passion, sex, drugs, rock 'n' roll and debauchery – and that's just the introduction where I talk about the press boys in the departure lounge! Little bit of humour there, although some of their offerings over the past decade should qualify for the Booker Prize for fiction.

I've been there, seen it and been arrested wearing the Bulldog Bobby T-shirt along with the other dodgy trio of Mad Monty, Crusher Chits and Strace the Ace. Tell me, what's selling in football nowadays? *Fever Pitch.* A book written by a middle-class trendy who took one slap outside Arsenal. We are talking about writing by the masses for the masses. We are talking Sun readers buying this by the barrow load.

What about this?

Chits shouted across the beer-stained bar.

'Oi, you frog-faced git, serve me a beer and make it quicker than you can shout "Je suis surrender, Mr Kraut".'

The barman scowled, but only briefly, as Chits smashed the ashtray across the side of his head, splitting it open. The blood spurted out, spraying the other horrified customers. Amidst the sound of smashing glasses and the stomach-churning noise of flesh being sliced by glass, the words 'Sacré bleu' were heard.

'Sacré bleu, you collaborators; it's us lot that saved you,' shouted Mad Monty, swigging his beer back in one gulp and then pitching the empty bottle at the prostrate groaning body of the hapless barman. The chant went up: 'We're doin' it for England, Engerland.'

There's plenty of that but more besides as the lads blaze a trail across Europe, finally ending up in the slammer where one of them becomes a reformed character thanks to the English language. I have been told that I have latent talent, so where do we take this?

Quick, throw a bucket of water over the printing presses to cool them down. I can see you salivating orgasmically at the prospect of taking this book. You will appreciate that I will need to write under a pseudonym, as I may still be wanted for certain crimes in Continental Europe.

I understand from my course that you usually offer a large advance for talented writers who have something to offer. Do I need to call in at the offices for a meeting? Do you wish to meet the other protagonists?

I await your offer.

The typewriter is ready.

Bill 'Bootsy' Egan

PS You're not related to 'Three Fingers' Harold Evans, are you, who drinks in the Three Bells just off the Euston Road?

Copies to: Andre Deutsch
            Transworld Publishers

ff

Faber and Faber Limited Publishers, 3 Queen Square, London WC1N 3AU

Mr Bill Egan
Guildford Road
Leatherhead
Surrey KT24 5NW

5 February 1997

Dear Mr Egan,

Many thanks for your letter of 1 February.

You would be very welcome to submit *Hooligan's Rough Guide to Europe*. So send it to me and I'll get back to you as soon as I can.

Yours sincerely,

Matthew Evans
Chairman

Andre Deutsch Ltd
106 Great Russell Street, London WC1B 3LJ

Mr William Egan
Guildford Road
Leatherhead
Surrey KT24 5NW

7 February 1997

Dear Bootsy,

Tom Rosenthal is away from the office so your blood-dripping proposal ripped across my desk. I am sure that you will soon establish unstoppable momentum, but I am afraid this one is not for us and I can only wish you well.

Yours sincerely,

Tim Forrester

Transworld Publishers Ltd
61–63 Uxbridge Road, London W5 5SA

Mr Bill Egan
Guildford Road
Leatherhead
Surrey KT24 5NW

4 February 1997

Dear Mr Egan,

Re: *Hooligan's Rough Guide to Europe*

Thank you for your letter to Mr Rubin about your book *Hooligan's Rough Guide to Europe*, which we have read with interest.

I'm sorry to disappoint you on this occasion but we don't feel that this is suitable for our list at Bantam Press, as we doubt we could make a commercial success of it. I'm afraid, due to the volume of submissions received, we are unable to expand upon this decision or the report leading to it.

Many thanks in any case for letting us consider your material and we wish you every success with your endeavours.

Yours sincerely,

Editorial Department

Guildford Road
Leatherhead
Surrey KT24 5NW

The Editor
The Guardian
119 Farringdon Road
London EC1R 3ER

1 February 1997

Dear Sir,

I demand that you dismiss Mr Frank Keating immediately following the disgusting writing in his column on Friday, 31 January 1997.

I enclose a letter I have sent to the DPP.

I await your reply on this matter.

Yours sincerely,

William Egan

Guildford Road
Leatherhead
Surrey KT24 5NW

Dame Barbara Mills
The Director of Public Prosecutions
The DPP's Office
50 Ludgate Hill
London EC4M 7EX

1 February 1997

Dear Dame Barbara,

I would like to draw your attention to the article which appeared in the Guardian on Friday, 31 January 1997 and demand that you take action under whatever law covers this disgraceful writing. As a football fan (and reformed boot boy) I have to accept that my right to free speech is curtailed for the common good. Like the rest of the lads I used to shout monkey noises and throw bananas with the best of them, but I'm politically correct with pictures of Wrighty up on the wall now.

Imagine my horror when I read Frank Keating's disgraceful piece about how he was covering the early fights of Mike Tyson, heavyweight champion of the world:

> I matily sucked up to one of his inner circle. What did he particularly notice
> in there when the demon Tyson was getting stripped for the contest?
> 'That Mike's got a surprisingly small dick,' he said, matter of fact.

Later on he talked about 'Wally? He liked a shag.'

Whilst this was reprehensible it was the gratuitous reference to the size of a black man's todger which was derogatory and racist. Correct me if I'm wrong, but if I shout out 'Wrighty, you've got a small dick' to Ian Wright at Highbury next time he misses an open goal, or 'Bergkamp, you're a Dutch woman's female reproductive organ', I think that one of the Metropolitan Police's finest will feel my collar.

For this offence I believe I could be fined £1,000. Only last season Mad Monty was dragged from his bed at dawn in front of a TV camera and his three Euro 96 match tickets were paraded in front of the camera as proof that he was planning the next campaign of football violence because he threw a plastic seat back at some Spurs fans when they were cutting up rough at Highbury.

For the record, it was Mr Keating who used this Friday column to try and denigrate the fact that Euro 96 was not the violent confrontation the press scribes predicted it would be. Not that I am advocating you prosecute as an act of revenge, but those who live by the sword must expect to die by it.

I look forward to your assurance that you intend to start proceedings in this case against Frank Keating and the Guardian. Failing that, I will have to look at going along to the press box next time he shows his face at Stamford Bridge to personally show my displeasure to Frank Keating. No doubt I will be able to cite any inactivity by the DPP as my defence.

Yours sincerely,

William Egan

Copies to: David Mellor MP
            Mrs Mary Whitehouse
            Hugh McIlvanney, Chief Sportswriter, The Sunday Times

The Guardian
119 Farringdon Road, London EC1R 3ER

William Egan
Guildford Road
Leatherhead
Surrey KT24 5NW

11 March 1997

Dear Mr Egan,

I have reread Mr Keating's piece, which seems to be not at all offensive. It was a piece of light writing which quoted a number of comments from sportsmen in the sort of robust language that sportsmen traditionally use.

I look forward to seeing what sort of response you get from the Director of Public Prosecutions.

Yours sincerely,

Alan Rusbridger
Editor

Guildford Road
Leatherhead
Surrey KT24 5NW

David Mellor MP
The House of Commons
London SW1A 0AA

1 February 1997

Dear Mr Mellor,

As a football fan I demand that you take this up in the House of Commons or, at the very least, give him a hard time on Radio Five Live.

I suppose Frank Keating will have a smug go at Chelsea's Italians next if he's allowed to get away with this.

I enclose a copy of the letter I have sent to the DPP.

Chelsea for Wembley.

William Egan

Guildford Road
Leatherhead
Surrey KT24 5NW

David Mellor MP
The House of Commons
London SW1A 0AA

8 March 1997

Dear Marshmellow,

I have received no reply to my letter dated 1 February. Do you only reply to letters when they are sent to the Daily Mirror? I must assume that you are paid per letter as that seems to be the way Parliament works, with cash for questions. Here's a fiver to help you pay for the notepaper before you are consigned to the opposite side of the terraces.

Anyway, my original letter is now very topical as I see Mr Schmeichel is about to get charged with calling Ian Wright black.

I wonder if you had more luck lip-reading Peter Schmeichel on Saturday at the Bridge than I did? I saw him say something to Ruud at the end but I missed it as the guy next to me was shouting obscenities at Roy Keane over a late tackle. It was so late it was the one he was aiming at Wrighty last Wednesday, but he caught Wisey instead.

Further to my original letter I am chasing up the DPP. I hope I can rely on you.

Get your best sailor suit out; Chelsea are off to inspect the Navy at Portsmouth next week.

William Egan

Enc. £5 note

The Rt. Hon. David Mellor QC MP
Member of Parliament for Putney
House of Commons, London SW1A 0AA

Mr William Egan
Guildford Road
Leatherhead
Surrey KT24 5NW

18 March 1997

Dear Mr Egan,

Thank you for your letter of 8 March. Unfortunately I did not receive your original letter – if I had I would most certainly have got back to you.

Please find returned your £5 note with my best wishes.

Yours sincerely,

(Dictated by David Mellor and signed in his absence)

National Viewers' and Listeners' Association
All Saints House, High Street, Colchester CO1 1UG

Mr W. Egan
Guildford Road
Leatherhead
Surrey KT24 5NW

10 February 1997

Dear Mr Egan,

Thank you for your letter of 1 February to Mrs Whitehouse. I am sorry to say that she is not well at the moment and not able to reply personally. Moreover, Mrs Whitehouse retired as our President in 1994.

I very much agree with your assessment of the item published in the Guardian. I fear that such things are not likely to be considered capable of successful criminal prosecution under the present law on obscenity. We have fought for many years to strengthen the law and we are hopeful that this will be achieved before much longer.

In these circumstances a private prosecution is not likely to be entertained by the Crown Prosecution Service, who must give consent to proceedings in these matters.

As I understand it the Press Complaints Commission will adjudicate on complaints only from people directly concerned. This would mean that Mike Tyson himself should send in a complaint.

I am sorry that we cannot be more helpful but I am sure that if you wrote to the editor of the Guardian in a constructive way, such offence may be avoided in the future.

I have pleasure in enclosing some information about our work which I trust will be of interest.

Yours sincerely,

John C. Beyer

Guildford Road
Leatherhead
Surrey KT24 5NW

The Director of Public Prosecutions
The DPP's Office
50 Ludgate Hill
London EC4M 7EX

24 February 1997

Dear Sir,

I have received no reply to my letter dated 1 February 1997. Are you going to do anything about the matter I raised? Or are you giving me *carte blanche* to go and punch this man in the teeth, citing your inactivity as a justification defence?

I note that the police are preparing a report for the CPS over the alleged comments made by Peter Schmeichel of Manchester United towards Ian Wright of Arsenal.

I await your reply on this most serious matter.

Yours sincerely,

William Egan

Guildford Road
Leatherhead
Surrey KT24 5NW

Dame Barbara Mills
The Director of Public Prosecutions
The DPP's Office
50 Ludgate Hill
London EC4M 7EX

17 March 1997

Dear Madam,

I have received no reply to my letters dated 1 February and 24 February 1997. Are you going to do anything about the matter I raised? Or are you giving me a Royal Charter to go and thrash this man to within an inch of his life, citing your inactivity as *provocation extremis*?

I note that the police are preparing a report for the CPS over the alleged comments made by Peter Schmeichel of Manchester United towards Ian Wright of Arsenal.

I have obviously missed the way the DPP does business in these cash-for-questions times, so I enclose $5 to help smooth your way to replying to this matter.

I await your reply on this most serious matter.

Yours sincerely,

William Egan

Enc. $5 US

CPS
Headquarters, 50 Ludgate Hill, London EC4M 7EX

Mr W. Egan
Guildford Road
Leatherhead
Surrey KT24 5NW

21 March 1997

Dear Mr Egan,

Thank you for your letter addressed to the Director of Public Prosecutions dated 17 March 1997. I am sorry to see that you did not have a reply to your letters of 1 and 24 February 1997, but it appears that this office did not receive them.

The Crown Prosecution Service is responsible for the review and, when appropriate, prosecution of allegations of crime which result from investigations by the police.

If you wish to make an allegation of crime, I would suggest that you consider making a report to your local police.

I hope the above is of assistance.

Yours sincerely,

Mr P. Cross
Casework Services Division

Guildford Road
Leatherhead
Surrey KT24 5NW

Dame Barbara Mills
The Director of Public Prosecutions
The DPP's Office
50 Ludgate Hill
London EC4M 7EX

22 March 1997

Dear Madam,

I have today received a reply from Mr P. Cross, Casework Services Division, regarding my original complaint about the disgusting article written in the Guardian. Well, I am extremely cross as well.

It seems that the DPP does not look into criminal activity unless the police give them the nod. No wonder no police ever get prosecuted for beating up football fans. I must assume the Portuguese police have the same *carte blanche*, which is why they beat the brains out of the Manchester United fans the other evening.

It is funny, because I swear that I read that the CPS twice asked Ian Wright if he wanted to press charges against Peter Schmeichel over alleged racist comments.

Perhaps you would be kind enough to pass my letters on to the relevant police authority so they can investigate my complaint.

I await confirmation that you have passed my original letters on, as you seem to be in the habit of conveniently losing letters from concerned football fans seeking equality under the law.

Yours sincerely,

William Egan

CPS

Headquarters, 50 Ludgate Hill, London EC4M 7EX

Mr W. Egan
Guildford Road
Leatherhead
Surrey KT24 5NW

2 April 1997

Dear Mr Egan,

Thank you for your letter dated 22 March 1997 addressed to the Director of Public Prosecutions, which has been passed to me for attention.

I have seen previous correspondence that you have sent to this office, but regret that I am able to add little more to Mr Cross's letter to you of 21 March 1997.

If you are concerned that a criminal offence has been committed, you may report it to your local police. It will be for the police to decide what action should be taken.

I am returning your previous correspondence so that should you wish to contact Surrey Police, you can refer your letters to them at the following address: Surrey Police, Mount Browne, Sandy Lane, Guildford GU3 1HG, tel: 01483 571212.

I hope that I have helped to clarify your position.

Yours sincerely,

R. Ashman (Miss)
Casework Services Division

Surrey Police
Police Headquarters, Mount Browne, Sandy Lane, Guildford, Surrey GU3
1HG

Mr W. Egan
Guildford Road
Leatherhead
Surrey KT24 5NW

30 April 1997

Dear Mr Egan,

Thank you for your letter enclosing the Guardian article. I have taken advice from our Criminal Investigation Department and have to tell you that the article does not breach the criminal law.

Surrey Police will, therefore, take no further action on this matter. You may wish to consult a solicitor with regard to civil action or contact the Press Complaints Commission.

Thank you for allowing me the opportunity to comment.

Yours sincerely,

Paul McElroy
Chief Inspector
Staff Officer to the Chief Constable

Guildford Road
Leatherhead
Surrey KT24 5NW

Nick Hornby
Author, Fever Pitch
c/o Victor Gollancz
Wellington House
125 The Strand
London WC2R 0BB

11 February 1997

Dear Fellow Gooner,

As an ex-Northbanker of no mean repute (alias 'Bootsy', amongst other fierce names), I am writing to you regarding your book, *Fever Pitch*, which I had the pleasure to read in the slammer.

I am a Gunner and proud as yourself, but I can't afford to move to Islington to be close to the Highbury Stadium shrine as all my security work is this side of the river. There is one disturbing aspect of the book which I must tug you about. In it you received a slap from a Yorkie (Leeds fan) and did nothing except whimper.

I understand horses for courses and writer not fighter, but I heard some lads talking about a film of the book the other night. I hope that this sequence is not repeated in the film, as I did not stand my ground on the Northbank against those George the Bears from east London, or appear in front of the beak to be fined, just to be portrayed on film as a supporter of 'wimpsville'.

I want your categorical assurance that Arsenal fans are not to be shown as wimps. Proud, passionate and sometimes a little outrageous, but wimps and cowards: NEVER, as Harry Enfield would put it.

I await your assurance on this serious matter.

East Stand rules.

Bring back the Northbank.

William Egan

Fever Pitch

Dear William Egan,

I don't think the film touches on the subject of wimps, really, so you don't need to feel ashamed. But, as you can tell, I'm a wimp myself, so I can't be sure.

Hope you enjoy it.

Nick Hornby

Guildford Road
Leatherhead
Surrey KT24 5NW

Francis Lee
Chairman
Manchester City Football Club
Maine Road
Manchester M14 7WN

21 February 1997

Dear Franny,

I would like to apply for the job of Manchester City Football Manager. I know that you have appointed the redoubtable Frank Clark but, like yourself, I do study the form in *The Sporting Life.*

Looking at the form, I would say that Frank would be lucky to last 12 months, so I would like to throw my hat in the ring early, so to speak. I think I have the answer to your problems. What you need is motivation for your players and that is where I come in.

Currently the players stroll around as if they will win games by right. It soon drove Steve Coppell to distraction. What you need is someone who will have the boys so fired up that they will put the fear of God into the opposition. Did you see what Brian Gayle of Wimbledon did to Frank Leboeuf of Chelsea the other week? Two bone-crunchers and a stray elbow and he was running around the pitch like the retreating French army. (Let's be fair; they've had plenty of practice.)

Motivation is my game. I learnt my trade in the hard school of knocks, so you know where I am coming from. Tactics is for the experts. I would appoint Don Howe to coach the boys into disciplined habits. At the moment I have motivated the lads near to the double of the Leatherhead Sunday League Division Seven league and cup. I have even got Strace the Ace back to his scoring best by limiting his Saturday night intake to ten pints!

I am in Manchester on Wednesday 26 February, so I could pop in to discuss terms, etc.

I await the call to arms.

NO REPLY

William Egan

71

Guildford Road
Leatherhead
Surrey KT24 5NW

Francis Lee
Chairman
Manchester City Football Club
Maine Road
Manchester M14 7WN

29 February 1997

Dear Franny,

I would just like to congratulate you on the sound appointment of Frank Clark. If ever there was a man who'll turn the tide against the red meanies the other side of Rainsville (that's what we call Manchester down here) then it's Frank. How do I know that? Because I saw him get the best out of Kevin Campbell down at Leyton Orient. Anybody who can do that is all right by me. By the time he got him back for Nottingham Forest it was too late to halt the malaise that had set in while working for George Graham. That man could turn Alan Shearer into a ten-goals-a-season man – at centre-half, of course.

I could also do with you having a few words for my son. Like yourself he looks like he'll only grow to 5ft 6ins tall, but he has a shot like a Royal Artillery howitzer and likes to get in where it hurts. I wonder if you have any words of encouragement for a fellow small 'un to help him along the way, although I would prefer you not to say anything about diving in the box. Crusher Chits's dad reckoned he saw you fouled near the half-way line at Stamford Bridge and you dived so far that when you finally touched land once again you were inside the goal net, and the referee gave you the penalty which you proceeded to rocket past the startled Peter Bonetti.

Your words of wisdom are awaited.

William Egan

Manchester City plc
Maine Road, Moss Side, Manchester M14 7WN

Mr William Egan
Guildford Road
Leatherhead
Surrey KT24 5NW

18 March 1997

Dear Mr Egan,

I wish to acknowledge your letter dated 29 February and, as you know, I have been a football supporter like yourself for many years.

There have been many footballers between about 5ft 4ins and 5ft 8ins; even the great Pele was only 5ft 8ins. Bobby Charlton was 5ft 7ins and Billy Bremner and Johnny Giles from Leeds were only tiddlers.

I believe that courage and desire override any height problems and there is no substitute for skill and ability. In fact, most of these smaller players tend to have a nasty streak!

Whilst writing, I would like to take this opportunity of thanking you for your continued and valued support.

Yours sincerely,

F.H. Lee
Chairman

Guildford Road
Leatherhead
Surrey KT24 5NW

Patrick Barclay
Chief Football Correspondent
The Sunday Telegraph
Peterborough Court at South Quay
181 Marsh Wall
London E14 9SR

24 February 1997

Dear Mr Barclay,

I am very disturbed by your lack of condemnation of Peter Schmeichel for racially abusing Ian Wright, but also for not castigating Manchester United, who should have thrown Peter into the North Sea and made him swim back to Denmark.

It seems as if the media have had a meeting and decided to blame Ian Wright for all the problems, even though Manchester seem to play in the mirror image of Alex Ferguson involved in a Govan shipyard kickabout.

Wrighty is just a humble south London black who doesn't take kindly to people calling him 'Sambo'. It would seem fair to expect the press to back him, but what does one expect when you vote Kung Fu Eric as Footballer of the Year?

If I were to call Ian Wright a black so-and-so, I would be hauled in front of the beak and banned from Highbury to Hillsborough. Schmeichel does it and you blame Ian Wright for being a hothead.

I would have thought you would have wanted to uphold the sterling traditions which your newspaper purports to represent. I expect you have a good explanation – like you hate Arsenal but love Manchester United.

I await your reply on this matter, or do you wish to discuss it in the Arsenal Tavern public house before the next Arsenal home game?

Gunner and proud,

William 'Bootsy' Egan

The Sunday Telegraph
I Canada Square, Canary Wharf, London E14 5AR

3 March 1997

Dear Bill,

Many thanks for your letter. If you read more carefully, you'll find no defence
of racial abuse. But I'll tell you what: I'd rather be called a black bastard, or a
bald bastard (which I am), or any other name than have my leg broken.
Wright's was the greater crime.

I'll see you in the Arsenal Tavern any time, by the way, just so long as it's an
individual game . . . and you're buying.

Best wishes,

Patrick Barclay

Guildford Road
Leatherhead
Surrey KT24 5NW

Richard Williams
Sportswriter
The Guardian
119 Farringdon Road
London EC1R 3ER

25 February 1997

Dear Richard,

I picked up my Guardian newspaper today expecting to read about how terrible it was for Ian Wright to be the subject of racist abuse. After all, you were the man who once wrote that Terry Venables should pick 2.3 black men for his England team because that was the ratio playing in the Football League.

So what do we get? Absolute silence – but that is only to be expected, because you were probably one of those who voted Kung Fu Eric as Footballer of the Year last year and then have the temerity to give some lads indulging in a little friendly fisticuffs the other Saturday at the Chesterfield v Nottingham Forest match a hard time in your column.

I'd say you were a bit of a hypocritical lowlife and I'd like to know how you justify this. Me and the lads, Crusher Chits, Mad Monty and Strace the Ace, reckon you need a lesson in applied fairness. As LBJ said of the Vietcong: 'Grab 'em by the balls and their hearts and minds will soon follow.'

We'd like to know why you are biased against Wrighty and expect an answer, or else we will shake you warmly by the throat when we see you in Poland for the next England match. No close-circuit TV there, mate.

Aggrieved of Surrey.

William 'Bootsy' Egan

The Guardian
119 Farringdon Road, London EC1R 3ER

12 March 1997

Dear Mr Egan,

I see you're so proud of your letter that you sent it to me twice! So I paid you the respect of reading it twice – which didn't make its sentiment much clearer.

Nevertheless, you are right to perceive some uncertainty in my attitude to Ian Wright. He scores some wonderful goals, but I find him a pretty rebarbative character – as a public person, that is. I have no idea what he's like as a private man, but to equate some of his actions with the Cantona/Selhurst incident is absurd (although I would not say the same of Cantona's assaults on some of his fellow players, e.g. John Polson).

Any time you want to take this conversation outside, in Poland or elsewhere, you are very welcome to try.

Yours sincerely,

Richard Williams

Guildford Road
Leatherhead
Surrey KT24 5NW

Gordon Taylor
Hon. Secretary
Professional Footballers Association
c/o 16 Lancaster Gate
London W2 3LW

1 March 1997

Dear Gordon,

As a man who understands what it is like to give and receive right-handers I am writing to you concerning the differing police actions taken over the two types of football. Grobbelaar takes an elbow at Plymouth, a couple of players have a bit of argy-bargy and plod is running on the pitch talking about sending reports to the CPS.

Have a full-scale brawl with the oval ball on the pitch and plod is sitting in the stands shouting 'Get a good one into his fat ugly head'. Look at Mark Jones of Ebbw Vale. In a fight that was infinitely better than Steve Collins v Nigel Benn but not as good as Ali v Frazier, he took 12 unanswered shots to the head and then walked off with his brawling partner – and not one word. Not only that but he goes to the High Court this week and gets to continue playing (or punching).

Had a couple of fans done this then the beak would have banned them from every ground *sine die*, as well as offering them an enforced stay of around six months at Her Majesty's pleasure. If Wrighty and Schmeichel had decided on this course of action instead of calling each other nasty names (CPS again involved), the press would have labelled it treasonable. Poor old Graham Kelly at Lancaster Gate would have forgotten his elocution lessons and started really whining by the time the press had finished.

What are your views on this?

Players should vote to bring back the terraces!

SENT POSTCARD

William Egan

78

Guildford Road
Leatherhead
Surrey KT24 5NW

Gordon Taylor, MA., B.Sc. (Econ)
Chief Executive
Professional Footballers Association
2 Oxford Court
Bishopsgate
Manchester M2 3WQ

19 March 1997

Dear Gordon,

I recently wrote you a letter regarding the persecution of footballers compared to rugby players (from either code). Today I received a postcard which didn't even have a scribble for a signature.

You have acknowledged receipt of my letter. Does this mean you are going to reply or do I have to feel honoured that a man who has passed a couple of exams can send pre-printed postcards?

It's no wonder that Wrighty feels he has to take the law into his own hands, as they obviously have a trade association chief executive who spends all of his time passing exams and none replying to letters.

I await your reply – or should that be your postcard?

William Egan

Professional Footballers Association
2 Oxford Court, Bishopsgate, Manchester M2 3WQ

Mr W. Egan
Guildford Road
Leatherhead
Surrey KT24 5NW

26 March 1997

Dear Mr Egan,

With reference to your letter of 19 March, we have a laid-down disciplinary code for players under the supervision of the FA and agreed with the PFA, and there is also a recommended code of conduct.

For incidents such as that involving Ian Wright and Peter Schmeichel where there are racist allegations, different attitudes have to be adopted with a view to improving race relations.

The disciplinary code in football is such that there has virtually never been any reference to a court to overturn any action against a player.

Yours sincerely,

Gordon Taylor
Chief Executive

Guildford Road
Leatherhead
Surrey KT24 5NW

Mr Ryszard Stemplowski
Polish Ambassador
Embassy of Poland
47 Portland Place
London W1N 3AG

8 March 1997

Dear Mr Stemplowski,

Myself and a few of the lads – Crusher Chits, Strace the Ace, Mad Monty – plus a couple of other assorted miscreants are due to visit your country in May for the football match against England. Good English boys with Union Jack underpants, you understand.

Last time we were there we heard the usual Polish jokes: What do you call a pretty girl in Poland? A tourist. What's 100 yards long and eats cabbage? A Polish meat queue. What do America and Poland have in common? You can't spend zlotys in either.

When we got to Poland we found that most of this was true, although we did find one or two pretty girls. However, one day Chits went out and looked in an empty shop and people started queuing behind him. Monty also had the unfortunate episode where he was arrested after taking a beating from a few of your boys, then had to pay a spot fine to your uniformed finest to get released to go to hospital.

I now look after the rich and famous and one of them informed me recently that the outlook in Poland is decidedly brighter on the economy front and the queues are only 25 yards long now. Please advise us so we can plan our itinerary properly and decide what to do with our surplus zlotys we brought home last time.

I await your reply on this matter.

William Egan

Guildford Road
Leatherhead
Surrey KT24 5NW

Mr Ryszard Stemplowski
Polish Ambassador
Embassy of Poland
47 Portland Place
London W1N 3AG

28 March 1997

Dear Mr Stemplowski,

I find it incredible that you haven't had the common decency to reply to my letter dated 8 March 1997 re the lads' visit to Poland for the World Cup qualifier in May.

I expect you were too busy telling your baton-wielding boys to get a view of the Portuguese plod bashing and machine-gunning the Mancunians.

Get a grip on yourself. When in London it is polite to reply to letters. I enclose $5 US to help you pay for the postage.

William Egan

Ambasada Rzeczypospolitej Polskiej
Embassy of the Republic of Poland
47 Portland Place, London W1N 3AG

Mr William Egan
Guildford Road
Leatherhead
Surrey KT24 5NW

1 April 1997

Dear Mr Egan,

With reference to your letter of 28 March 1997, I would like to let you know that we have not received your first letter dated 8 March.

Since it happens from time to time, we have found the tone of your letter of 28 March exceptionally rude.

Enclosed please find your $5 US. There are a great number of charities in this country and we suggest you support one of them.

Yours sincerely,

A. Kolczynski
Counsellor

Guildford Road
Leatherhead
Surrey KT24 5NW

Mr Galli Paolo
Italian Ambassador
Embassy of Italy
143 Kings Yard
London W1Y 2EH

8 March 1997

Dear Mr Paolo,

Myself and a few of the lads, Crusher Chits, Strace the Ace and Mad Monty, are currently planning our trip to Rome for the return match of the World Cup qualifiers in October this year. However, we don't know whether we should book a single ticket or a return trip.

Last time Monty was there for Italia 90 he was having a quiet lager in Rimini when he was duffed up by a mob in uniform, held on a petrol station forecourt, and then shipped home unceremoniously on an airliner with 300 other lads. Funny how there didn't seem to be any spare seats on the airliner. You must have tremendous salespeople out there!

That's the reason for writing. We just wanted to know if the government of Italy are going to arrange an airliner home again? If they are then we won't waste our money booking a return trip, we'll just take four of the seats under the Italian pre-booking scheme.

As you can't possibly be as lucky in Rome as you were at Wembley, we will be celebrating in full Peroni mode.

Arrivederci Italia.

France here we come!

NO REPLY

William Egan

Guildford Road
Leatherhead
Surrey KT24 5NW

John Prescott
Deputy Leader
Labour Party
The House of Commons
London SW1A 0AA

8 March 1997

Dear Fellow Red,

A disturbing trend has emerged which could yet deny you your place at the trough. Do you note how the Tory mob are climbing on the backs of the blues boys down the Kings Road? If David 'The Gap' Mellor isn't being a man of the people at Stamford Bridge, then it's John Boy standing there with his man-of-the-people grin. I doubt if it was lost on you that Chelsea (the blues) came back from a hopeless deficit against Liverpool (the reds) to turn the tide and win the other week.

What you need is a reds-supporting man in London, and that means Arsenal. What have you currently got? Roy 'Sheffield Wednesday' Hattersley – a team who are called 'the Owls' and play in stripes. No, what you need is a high-profile man at the Gunners. You can even be European and shake hands with Dennis Bergkamp.

Football's where it's at. Don't think for one minute that John won't be at the next big Chelsea cup-tie with a grin as wide as the Blackwall Tunnel. It's his only chance. Don't let him steal the football card at the last minute. Do you think he cares about the World Cup or football? I didn't see Johnny Major or any of those other Tories sticking up for football when Maggie 'I hate football' Thatcher was in power. Now they are falling over themselves to get the footie freebies.

Come on you reds.

NO REPLY

William Egan

Guildford Road
Leatherhead
Surrey KT24 5NW

Paddy Ashdown
Leader
Liberal Democrat Party
The House of Commons
London SW1A 0AA

8 March 1997

Dear Fellow Marine,

I am writing to you over a policy you are missing, one which could enhance your election prospects. Football is big news, and currently enjoys a very high profile.

Do you note how the Tory mob are climbing on the success of the Chelsea blues boys down the Kings Road? You can't get into Chelsea nowadays without tripping over a fawning Tory politician. If David 'The Gap' Mellor isn't copping a photo opportunity at Stamford Bridge, then it's John Boy standing there with his honest-mate-I-understand-the-people grin. Let's be fair; he thinks the ECU is a new foreign player Ruud Gullit is about to sign. I doubt it was lost on a worldly man like yourself that Chelsea (the blues) recently came back from a hopeless 2–0 deficit against Liverpool (the reds) to turn the tide and win 4–2.

Labour have got their football man, Roy 'Sheffield Wednesday' Hattersley – a team who reflect the working-class origins of iron and steel – while the Liberal Democrats have got? Zilch.

What you need is to be seen supporting a football team who represent your image: proud, dependable Paddy. So you obviously can't be seen supporting Arsenal, whose players seem to have every vice known to man, plus a few more.

No, the team you need to be seen watching is Fulham. Once in the First Division but a nice bunch of guys and definitely on the way back up. Being seen at football is now *de rigueur*, but whoever is advising you is way off the pace of the ball. Get down to Craven Cottage, but don't forget to mention it to all the press first so you are seen at the match.

Up the Fulham.

William Egan

Liberal Democrats
Party Headquarters, 4 Cowley Street, London SW1P 3NB

William Egan
Guildford Road
Leatherhead
Surrey KT24 5NW

14 April 1997

Dear Mr Egan,

Thank you for the letter addressed to Paddy Ashdown. He is very grateful to you for taking the trouble to write to him and has asked me to reply.

Your letter makes some very interesting points and these will be noted. In view of the pressure of the general election campaign, I am afraid we cannot reply to your letter at greater length. Nevertheless, we are most grateful to you for writing and letting Mr Ashdown know of your views.

Best wishes.

Yours sincerely,

Phyllis Ballantyne
Liberal Democrat Correspondence Unit

Guildford Road
Leatherhead
Surrey KT24 5NW

Jeff Powell
Chief Sportswriter
The Daily Mail
Northcliffe House
2 Derry Street
Kensington
London W8 5TT

8 March 1997

Dear Jeff,

I have received no reply to my letter dated 28 October 1996. Don't worry, we haven't forgotten you. We are still intending to travel to Poland, especially now that our presence becomes more imperative by the hour. Somebody has to support the lads.

We are hoping to present you with the special award, so we just need your OK that you will meet us. Perhaps you can arrange a photo shoot to show off your famous sense of humour?

All the lads are in expectation of meeting you.

I await your reply.

William Egan

NO REPLY

Guildford Road
Leatherhead
Surrey KT24 5NW

Sam Hamman
Owner
Wimbledon Football Club
Selhurst Park Stadium
London SE25 6PY

8 March 1997

Dear Sam,

Magic, mate, you are stuffing them faster than a Bernard Matthews worker, but do we smell a conspiracy? Firstly they make you go to Old Trafford, then they send you away again to the Steely Dans from Sheffield. I don't think the establishment have forgiven you for beating Liverpool in the FA Cup final. But who cares, as the 'Crazy Gang' are equipped to survive. I even heard Alan Hansen praising you.

However, a note of caution. In the moment of glory against the Manchester United red menace at Selhurst, Vinnie Jones was swapping blows with Mick Harford. Where is he at? I believe you once called him 'Mosquito Brain'. Have a quiet word or paint the dressing-rooms at Selhurst a pastel pink, as this calms people down.

The problem you will face is that when you start to get famous the knockers will start to get down on you. Incidents like that will have the popular press demanding that Vinnie be hung by his whatnots from the Tower.

I wonder if you could say a few words to my son who seems to think that crashing into tackles like a demented madman is the 'Wimbledon way'. I keep trying to tell him that Wimbledon have now learnt how to play football, although I am prepared to be contradicted.

I await your reply on this matter.

A Crazy Ganger but not a Don.

William 'Bootsy' Egan

Wimbledon Football Club Ltd
Selhurst Park Stadium, London SE25 6PY

Mr William 'Bootsy' Egan
Guildford Road
Leatherhead
Surrey KT24 5NW

11 March 1997

Dear Bootsy,

Sam has asked me to write to you for your telephone number. It appears that Directory Enquiries do not have a number listed for you.

Perhaps you could be kind enough to phone me so that I can pass the number on to Sam.

Sincerely,

Stephanie Wilkes
Secretary to Sam Hamman

Guildford Road
Leatherhead
Surrey KT24 5NW

Sam Hamman
Owner
Wimbledon Football Club
Selhurst Park Stadium
London SE25 6PY

15 March 1997

Dear Sam,

Now you're gonna believe my theory that there is an establishment conspiracy against Wimbledon. To win the FA Cup this time you've got to beat them all.

Anyway, thanks for the letter from Stephanie Wilkes. I have left the number with Stephanie (she sounds a bit of all right, my old shipmate). Of course you can't find my number in Directory Enquiries, because it's ex-directory, like all the real stars of stage, screen and public bar. You can't be too careful nowadays. I bet you can't look up Vinnie Jones, Fash the Bash, yourself or that bird on page three with the huge bazoombas in the telephone directory.

I only wanted a couple of lines from you to my son to talk him out of trying to impersonate Vinnie, who now thinks he's going to be a film star.

Anyway, now we're going to talk on the phone, and perhaps have afternoon tea, you can reserve me two of the best next to you at Highbury, where together we can watch the Dons give those Kings Road tarts a memory which will enable them to tell their children about the day they met real men.

Look forward to the call.

Should the Dons come on to the pitch to the tune 'Crazy' by Patsy Cline or 'Mama We're All Crazy Now' by Slade?

William 'Bootsy' Egan

Sent telephone number to Sam

Sam left message on ansaphone:
'Hello, Bootsy, are you rich?'

Guildford Road
Leatherhead
Surrey KT24 5NW

John Lewis
Headmaster
Eton College
Eton
Berkshire

8 March 1997

Dear John,

Yours is a college which attracts the rich, the famous and the future rulers of the world. Every part of their education is catered for, but I believe one burgeoning area is being sadly overlooked. Read the financial pages and what is big business? Football. Never a day goes past without the city queuing up to get their snouts in the football trough. Today AC Milan are looking for a £500 million stock-market listing. Your lads will be left behind if they miss out on a football education.

What your boys need is coaching in the finer arts of the real game of Association Football – and not just the playing arts, but the whole shebang of foul play, stray elbows and how to spot players who like the odd line of charlie.

That is where I come in. I've served my time at the sharp end alongside one or two ex-internationals, but now I've discovered a new lease of life and want to show your lads how understanding football is the key to success for the next millennium. Show me somebody who doesn't like football and I'll show you a loser.

I can offer my services to your college as roving soccer coach, able to impart the finer points to your lads. I can even teach them the refined art of slapping the nut if you deem it correct.

It's a tough world out there, so you will be doing your charges a service if you prepare them fully. I am only available on Monday and Wednesday afternoons for coaching, as my security work takes up the rest of my time. Do you want me to pop in for an informal chat and introduce a couple of the lads who are prepared to help me out?

Your man with the FA coaching manual and the unwritten tactics book!

NO REPLY

William 'Bootsy' Egan

Guildford Road
Leatherhead
Surrey KT24 5NW

Bryan Robson
Manager
Middlesbrough Football Club
Riverside Stadium
Middlesbrough TS3 6RS

15 March 1997

Dear Bryan,

What a revelation you are. How nice to see someone in the Premiership have the courage of another man's wallet to get in all those lovely foreigners to grace the North-east. Miserable, depressed and freezing cold up there. Yes, of course it is. It is a well-known fact down here in London that when it is warm down here it is still only two degrees above freezing up there. I know that sort of thing doesn't stop the locals walking around with just their shirt sleeves on, but what the heck.

What a great idea to warm the place up by importing foreigners with natural suntans. It might not be any warmer but by bringing in Brazilians and Italians you change people's perceptions about the place. I assume that is why the Brazilian chap came here. You showed him a picture of Middlesbrough in the middle of winter and everybody had just a T-shirt on so he thought it was warm! Great psychology and something a few more of our top-line managers should be looking at. Even though you are bottom of the league and sinking fast, everybody feels good about it.

You have obviously not spent enough, as you may only need another £21 million to make a real fist of it. I like the way you got those underpaid English players, like Craig Hignett, to take a cut in pay of £50 per week to enable that marvellous Ravanelli to be paid £40k per week. That sort of thing will make English players hungry – although we don't want them too hungry, as inability to afford basic carbohydrate will affect the English guys' ability to run around so that Ravanelli can tap them in from five yards, then sprint around like a headless chicken with his shirt over his head.

Mind you, in the final of the Coca-Cola Cup you will be facing proper bricklayer types from Wimbledon or Leicester, and I must warn you that if it's

Leicester they will have Mr Englishman, Captain hod carrier himself, Steve Claridge. Watch him very carefully, as his main method of scoring is to lull defenders into thinking that he's so crap that people don't have to bother. Foreigners fall for that. Remember the Trojans and that wooden horse thingy. They had great-looking women plus suntans, but conceded a late goal to the Greeks.

Get back to me if you need any further advice about foreigners, as I've had security experience in dodgy Tenerife night-clubs.

You didn't bring in those foreign players so you could eye up their girlfriends, did you? After all, any Englishman nicknamed Captain Marvel, as you were, must be a little warm blooded.

Your man doing the lambada!

William Egan

Middlesbrough Football Club
Cellnet Riverside Stadium, Middlesbrough TS3 6RS

William Egan
Guildford Road
Leatherhead
Surrey KT24 5NW

4 April 1997

Dear William,

Thank you for your letter to Bryan Robson which has been passed to me for reply.

Bryan thanks you for your comments, which have been noted, and sends his best wishes.

We hope we can count on your continued support of Middlesbrough Football Club.

Yours sincerely,

Diane O'Connell
Public Relations Officer

Guildford Road
Leatherhead
Surrey KT24 5NW

Private and Confidential

Sir Ian MacLaurin
Chairman English Cricket Board
c/o Tesco Stores Ltd
Cheshunt
Herts EN8 9SL

15 March 1997

Dear Sir Ian,

I read a disturbing article in the Daily Mail this week about the new direction of English cricket with which you are seemingly in agreement. It seems that the English cricket lads are to be discouraged from growing stubble and are to present themselves a little better. They are to be sent on management development courses to teach them about the importance of image and train them in how to make the most of their TV appearances.

Well, unless you've had your head in the sand or been taken in by too much belief in your ability to sell vegetables to the masses, then it might have escaped your notice that we are playing the Aussies next time – a team fresh from eyeballing the West Indies and making them blink.

This is a team which sends players over like David Boon, who drinks 47 cans of Fosters on the flight from Sydney, then doesn't shave for three weeks and occupies his crease for most of the tour while the English pace attack grovels. Another is Merv 'The Swerve' Hughes, whose under-nose tickler never stopped him sticking a fearsome bouncer under any poor Englishman's throat whenever he felt like reminding the crims back down under that all Poms are poofs.

Did you know that Aussies have a pastime called 'sledging', where they humiliate Poms by mocking their foibles? 'Hello, lads, had tuition in how to walk to the wicket, you poofy git?' It will be First Division humiliation.

Take a leaf from Terry Venables and football. Get the boys out to Hong Kong, ripping each others' shirts off and squirting vodka down the throat in a dentist's chair, then send the press releases to Shane Warne (and the rest of the

Aussies) with the message: 'Stand by to have your poofy pinkie broken again.' Send the boys on a night out with Gazza, but management courses? Give England a break.

At least Phil Tufnell looks like he could stand toe to toe with the Aussies in a beer-drinking contest.

Bring back Jabba the Hutt Gatting!

Support football. A man's game.

William Egan

From the Office of the Chairman
Lord MacLaurin of Knebworth
Tesco plc, Tesco House, Delamare Road, Cheshunt, Herts EN8 9SL

William Egan Esq.
Guildford Road
Leatherhead
Surrey KT24 5NW

19 March 1997

Dear Mr Egan,

I thank you for the letter of 15 March, which I enjoyed immensely. You
have put me in a most difficult position, as I thought I might be able to
improve the international players by sending them to the Royal Ballet
School, but I suppose this would not meet with your approval!

I wish you a great season.

Yours sincerely,

Ian MacLaurin

Guildford Road
Leatherhead
Surrey KT24 5NW

Arsène Wenger
Manager
Arsenal Football Club
Arsenal Stadium
Highbury
London N5 1BU

15 March 1997

Dear Arsène,

Nice move to change your name, but why not go the whole hog and add the 'al' instead of the 'e'? I suppose it is the Gallic flair we love to read about.

Now down to brass tacks about what is going on at Arsenal. First you come to Arsenal saying that you prefer 4:4:2, then you continue to play with the 5:3:2 Bruce Rioch formation. At the same time the Dutch start playing with four at the back and the other night I see your old mob, Monaco, and they are playing a fluid 4:4:2. Confused? Just a little. I wonder if the Arsenal players are. Perhaps you are a thinking man's Bruce Rioch.

Then I pick up the paper to read that you are giving the players creatine and orange juice for breakfast. I know that the average footballer is a bit thick, but do they know that they are taking an unproved protein extract? As a man who's done a bit of cycling at the sharp end (I love to give the elbow out at 30mph in a tight finish), I know about these things. I also do a bit of security work and I see plenty of these musclebound, pill-popping steroid-takers. Trust me, mate, they all end up with shrunken todgers and high-pitched voices. Perish the thought that that should happen to Tony Adams.

Whatever you do, keep the boys off the steroids and especially the EPO blood doping, which a lot of Dutch cyclists use. We don't want them suddenly dropping dead. However, the ideas about stretching are great. You move like a disciple of Tai Chi, which I assume you studied in the Far East.

I would be interested in your views on movement and whether the creatine story is true or whether it is just fabrication by another jealous tabloid journalist. By the way, your 3–0 prediction for Monaco v Newcastle was one out and I lost a fiver!

A thinker like yourself,

William Egan

Arsenal Football Club plc
Arsenal Stadium, Highbury, London N5 1BU

William Egan
Guildford Road
Leatherhead
Surrey KT24 5NW

24 March 1997

Dear Mr Egan,

Thank you for your recent letter and for your various comments, which have been noted.

Whilst I have read your views with interest, I am afraid that I do not wish to discuss individual players or team tactics at the present time, but can assure you that your loyal support is much appreciated by everyone at Highbury – let's all hope the club will have a successful future.

Many thanks, once again, for taking the trouble to write, and in closing I send you my very best wishes.

Yours sincerely,

Arsène Wenger
Manager

Guildford Road
Leatherhead
Surrey KT24 5NW

Sir James Goldsmith
Leader
The Referendum Party
1st Floor, Dean Bradley House
52 Horsferry Road
London SW1P 2AF

15 March 1997

Dear Fellow Englishman,

I recently received a personal message from yourself so I thought I would give you the benefit of some sound electoral advice which will help you get more votes and enhance your election prospects. Football is where every full-blooded Englishman should be at the present time – get on board.

Do you note how the political mob, especially the Tories, are leeching on the backs of the Chelsea blues boys down the Kings Road? If David 'Toesucker' Mellor isn't being Uncle Smarmy himself at Stamford Bridge (in between dating floosies), then it's John Boy Major (the ninth Walton: 'Goodnight, John Boy') standing there with his honest-mate-I-hated-Maggie-Thatcher's-poll-tax-but-I-was-only-following-orders grin.

Have you noticed how Chelsea, along with the rest of English football, are importing foreign players like crazed shopaholics? The media keep telling us what a great move it is for English football (the same media who tell us the EC is good for us), but what happens the other night? England lose their first ever home World Cup qualifier to a foreign team. Why, I ask? Because our Englishness is being diluted by misguided attempts to become European.

Even Labour have got their football man: Roy 'Sheffield Wednesday' Hattersley – a team who are importing anybody with a foreign-sounding name which doesn't reflect the working-class origins of iron and steel. Mind you, they got their comeuppance when they met the true-Brit English Wimbledon the other day.

You've got the basics right. Your address sounds like a 1960s full-back who used to kick opposing wingers over the stand and get a pat on the back from the referee for his trouble. Try that nowadays on those foreigners who roll around like they've been hit by a sniper if they are breathed on . . . poor old Dean Bradley would get banned while still protesting his innocence!

What you need is to be seen supporting football to show the English people that you understand the working man's hopes and aspirations. Better still, see if you can find one team with British ideals. The ethos of what you are proposing must be reflected in football. Ban all of these foreign players unless they agree to learn the words of 'Land of Hope and Glory' and 'Rule Britannia', which should be sung before all English football matches.

Football fans understand that. You can't afford not to be seen at the semi-final between little old English Chesterfield against European Middlesborough at Old Trafford next month.

If you are serious about getting into power you must get on board the football bandwagon. Chelsea have a dodgy-looking Dutch guy with dreadlocks and he is alleged to be sex mad (News of the World said he is seeing a 19-year-old bit of crumpet and seeing a sex therapist at the same time). This foreign manager is giving away our hard-earned pounds to enable ageing Italian players, considered too expensive for Italian football, to have a twilight benefit and a new villa on the Med.

Get back to me. I'm available for consultation on security and speechwriting advice.

There'll always be an England.

NO REPLY

William 'England' Egan

Guildford Road
Leatherhead
Surrey KT24 5NW

Alan Sugar
Chairman
Tottenham Hotspur Football Club
White Hart Lane
748 High Road
Tottenham
London N17 0AP

15 March 1997

Dear Alan,

Once again you seem to be getting worse press than Michael Jackson. Is it because you always seem so aggressive or is it the Essex man nose which could get you an audition for a part as a Bond film baddie? Or is there something else? Still, as a dyed-in-the-wool north London guy it doesn't matter to me whether or not you stick to your fiscal policies, the main thing is the team.

Quite how you managed to take the duffings at Bolton and Newcastle with the players you have at the club is beyond me, but the stick being levelled at yourself by the tabloids (and even the broadsheets) is a little too much.

I don't know about yourself but I am sick and tired of Spurs and Amstrad being the butt of all those northern sportswriters' jokes, so I am writing to offer you the services of the north London protection team. At the next shareholders' meeting we will duff up anybody who doubts your word.

I will put my cards on the table and say that I am an Arsenal fan, but, like you, I can see an earner. Forgive me if I too have a good laugh at your plight, but business is business – sentiments me and Jürgen understand only too well.

From what I have heard you need a few plants in the audience to stand up and state how you are constantly on the mobile during breaks in big-money Amstrad board meetings trying to sign players (I have read that it is a favourite tactic of Mr Grecian 2000 down the road, David Dein), but not flighty Krauts – for Jürgen Klinsmann read Jürgen Grabsthemoneyman – who fly back at the first offer of deutschmarks.

103

Or you can forget that. Just call in myself and a few of the lads who made their name in the real world. 'Insult Sugar and you insult Spurs. Take that, you spotty Bill Gates lookalike.' With that we can dish the bossocks and help them outside head first.

Our credentials are impeccable. Strace the Ace has done a ten for wounding with intent, Crusher Chits did a five for an attack on a rival pub and Frenchy has two 'not guiltys' at the Bailey. Step out of line in front of that lot if you dare, mate, eh?

Don't bring back Ossie Ardiles.

Yours sincerely

NO REPLY

William Egan

PS Did you ever drink in the Retreat, Chigwell Row?

Guildford Road
Leatherhead
Surrey KT24 5NW

Gary Lineker
Football Focus
Television Centre
White City
London

18 March 1997

Dear Gary,

You're a disgrace. Bland, boring and so on the fence your arse must be sore.

When are you going to really rip into somebody and stop being a jelly fish?

Yours sincerely,

William Egan

Gary Lineker

Mr William Egan
Guildford Road
Leatherhead
Surrey KT24 5NW

25 March 1997

Dear Mr Egan,

Thank you for your letter of 18 March. May I congratulate you on your vituperation.

Yours sincerely,

Gary Lineker

Guildford Road
Leatherhead
Surrey KT24 5NW

Private and Confidential

Ally McCoist
Glasgow Rangers Football Club
Ibrox Stadium
Glasgow

22 March 1997

Dear Ally,

Myself and Mad Monty currently have a bet which I would like you to settle. We reckon that you are fatter than 'Tubbs' Gazza and also slower in a sprint over 50 yards.

We also reckon that you and Gazza have gut-barging competitions during breaks in drinking, sorry, training – just a slip of the tongue. For your information, gut-barging is a game like Sumo where people barge into each other using their well-developed stomachs.

The bet is that you are at least 5lbs heavier than Gazza, so I wonder if you could confirm or deny this. Please don't be offended about this bet as you are far better looking, but then even John Wark could probably pull more birds than Gazza on a lads disco ensemble.

Here's a fiver as your cut of the bet I am about to win.

William Egan

Enc. An old £5 note but still legal tender

PS I once played against someone who played alongside you at Sunderland reserves, but don't worry – I kicked him right over the stands after ten minutes and I never saw him again for the rest of the match.

Dear Willie and Mad Monty,

Due to the fact that I am, at last weigh-in, grossly heavier than the fat Geordie, I am sitting down while I write this. I am, in my defence, five yards quicker in 50 yards and have far more ability in pulling birds than both he and John Wark combined.

Your £5 has been well spent on a double whopper and fries with a vanilla ice shake.

Yours in sport,

Ally McCoist

Guildford Road
Leatherhead
Surrey KT24 5NW

David Dein
Chief Executive
Arsenal Football Club
Arsenal Stadium
Highbury
London N5 1BU

22 March 1997

Dear David,

I read a disturbing article in the News of the World the other Sunday. It seems that Arsène Wenger is lacing the lads' drinks with creatine, an unproved protein extract designed to give more muscle power. On top of this, all I seem to read about is the newfangled fancy pasta-with-everything diets. It seems that diet makes you play.

Correct me if I'm wrong, but haven't Arsenal employed Liam 'Chippy' Brady, who in his heyday was called this because he ate more chips than the legendary Alf Tupper, hero of the Victor comic, the tough of the track who could have beaten Seb Coe and Steve Ovett in the same afternoon between plates of chips!

Spam and chips FA Cup final 1978, Pasty and chips FA Cup final 1979, smoked salmon, Chablis and chips FA Cup and Cup-Winners' Cup finals 1980. That was the order of the day.

It seems to me that Liam's dietary divergence didn't stop Arsenal fans remembering 'Chippy' Brady as one of the all-time greats before being transferred to Italy (Chianti and chips). As this might have been before your time, I will remind you that on a balmy 1980 April evening in Turin, Liam single-handedly destroyed Juventus in the Stadio Communiale, and was then asked to sign for them. Do you think they asked him if he ate pasta? Of course they didn't; they were more interested in whether he could play – which he jolly well could.

Liam didn't get where he was in football by watching his diet, as he knew that if you trained hard enough it didn't matter what you ate. A load of old tosh

108

is being spoken about diet, but ability and desire come from inside the heart, not the stomach. It would seem as if all this obsession with diet is hiding the fact that Arsenal haven't produced a half-decent player since Liam upped sticks for the lure of lira.

Please confirm that the emphasis at Arsenal is still being placed upon skill and not on fancy diets to help players run a bit longer or extra protein so we can outmuscle Wimbledon.

A fellow Arsenal fan but with less need of the Grecian 2000,

William 'Tough of the Track' Egan

Arsenal Football Club plc
Arsenal Stadium, Highbury, London N5 1BU

William Egan
Guildford Road
Leatherhead
Surrey KT24 5NW

14 April 1997

Dear Mr Egan,

Thank you for your letter of 22 March to David Dein regarding player diets.

There are one or two points I should like to make to put your mind at rest on this issue. Firstly, creatine is not designed to give more muscle power, nor is it unproven. It helps recovery after physical exercise and is widely used all over the Continent as an energy booster. My advice is to be very sceptical of newspaper articles more interested in writing supposedly scandalous headlines than in portraying the facts.

Secondly, I believe you have written to Liam Brady on this subject as well. I have also discussed your opinions with him and he feels that any methods a player can adopt to ensure optimum performance should be given careful consideration. Players' diets have received a great deal of coverage over the past few years as older pros realise that they can lengthen their playing careers by careful attention to such details.

Lastly, I would like to agree wholeheartedly with your points about ability and desire. I should also like to assure you that both Arsène Wenger and Liam agree with you as well! The spirit of our squad has been well documented over the past decade and this is something which has particularly impressed the manager. There will never be a substitute for skill and no amount of correct eating habits will replace hard work, dedication and practice to improve the skills a player is naturally blessed with.

Yours sincerely,

Clare Tomlinson
Head of Communications

Guildford Road
Leatherhead
Surrey KT24 5NW

Jeff Powell
Chief Sportswriter
The Daily Mail
Northcliffe House
2 Derry Street
Kensington
London W8 5TT

22 March 1997

Dear Jeff,

What are you on? Do you have psychological problems? I picked up my copy of the Daily Mail today expecting to read the strongest condemnation of the Portuguese authorities after they machine-gunned helpless Manchester United fans whose only crime was to want to travel to see a match which was already over at 4–0 from the first leg.

Perhaps their wish to travel in their thousands to watch a meaningless match made the Portuguese authorities think they were mentally subnormal? It could be that this is the way they treat mental defectives in Portugal? You might wish to pass these thoughts on to your investigative journalism department, if it has anybody left who isn't trying to dig dirt on Cherie Blair!

I expected to read 'Send in the Gunboats', 'Give Them the Cold Steel Back via the SAS' or 'Open Fire Back on the Algarve Bullies', but what do I read instead? A party political jibe at the Labour party over their proposal that they might think about bringing back terraces, plus a tasteless reference to Hillsborough.

Are you taking a backhander from John Major or does your editor instruct you to include digs about the Labour party in every article? It would have been different had the Bully Boys been dishing it out in the press box. Desmond Hackett (a proper journalist of the old school) must be turning in his grave.

I await your reply on this grave matter.

William Egan

NO REPLY

Copies to: Hugh McIlvanney, Chief Sportswriter, The Sunday Times
             Martin Edwards, Chief Executive, Manchester United

Guildford Road
Leatherhead
Surrey KT24 5NW

John Redwood MP
The House of Commons
London SW1A 0AA

28 March 1997

Dear John,

Felt I had to drop you a line over your Eurosceptic stand. The lads and I had a chat the other night and we want to know what your views on European football are. We believe that there is a sinister plot to subvert the English Football League and end up playing a Euro league thingy with the winners getting free entry into a corrupt society.

Look at our best players since the Europeans have come in. Tackle one of them and they go down like they've been hit by a Frank Bruno haymaker. Bribery and corruption, it's all there in large doses, every time a foreigner gets into English football and brown envelopes are passed around. Marseilles only won the European Cup because they bribed almost everybody (except the Conservative party, as it seems that Al Fayed was doing that), including a Swiss referee.

I saw a report on BBC's 'Football Focus' last Saturday which said that ten English teams could qualify for Europe. I believe that this, along with all these foreign players, is ruining the English game. Your views on Europe must be seen to include football or else these foreigners will overrun us.

Get back to me as quickly as you can so the lads can start lobbying their MPs about scaling down European competition. I don't want to switch on my TV next season to see some half-wit jock pundit like Alan Hansen telling me how good foreigners are at running off the ball. I was brought up to believe that all they do is run; they don't need a ball for that. Did you know that they want to put the English Premiership runners-up in the Champions League? Surely there is something wrong with that?

England is best.

Down with Europe.

William 'Bootsy' Egan

The Rt. Hon. John Redwood, MP
House of Commons, London SW1A 0AA

W. Egan Esq.
Guildford Road
Leatherhead
Surrey KT24 5NW

3 April 1997

Dear Mr Egan,

Thank you for your letter. As there is a parliamentary convention that Members of Parliament deal only with matters raised by their own constituents, I am sending your letter to your own Member of Parliament who, I am sure, will wish to reply to you.

Yours sincerely,

John Redwood

Guildford Road
Leatherhead
Surrey KT24 5NW

Malcolm Rifkind
Foreign Secretary
Foreign and Commonwealth Office
London SW1E 5HE

28 March 1997

Dear Mr Rifkind,

I enclose the letter I have written to the Italian Ambassador. (I have sent it twice but they keep sending it back. I have tried bribes but they just keep the money.) After the events in Portugal where the Portuguese police machine-gunned the unarmed women and children from Manchester United, I think it is pertinent. Their only crime? To watch Manchester United. OK, so Chits and Monty think it's a crime to want to watch Manchester United, but it isn't a shooting offence – yet!

What is the British government's position on protection of football fans abroad? It seems obvious that the Italians are shaping up to give the lads a bit of a thrashing when we go there in October.

William Egan

Enc. Letter dated 8 March addressed to Italian Ambassador

Foreign and Commonwealth Office
Consular Division, 1 Palace Street, London SW1E 5HE

William Egan Esq.
Guildford Road
Leatherhead
Surrey KT24 5NW

16 April 1997

Dear Mr Egan,

Thank you for your letter of 28 March to Malcolm Rifkind, which has been passed to me for reply.

We are committed to protecting the interests of all British nationals abroad. British football supporters are offered at least the same level of assistance as other British nationals who encounter problems when travelling abroad. I enclose a copy of our 'British Consular Services Abroad' leaflet for your information.

We have received no intelligence to suggest the Italian police will behave in an untoward manner to British supporters when they travel to Italy for the match on 11 October. However, we would expect all England supporters to behave correctly and to comply with local laws and customs during their stay in Italy as we would any other British visitor.

I cannot comment on the lack of response to your letters to the Italian Embassy.

Yours sincerely,

Mrs Angela Beuden
Consular Division

Guildford Road
Leatherhead
Surrey KT24 5NW

Peter Johnson
Chairman
Everton Football Club
Goodison Park
Liverpool L4 4EL

2 April 1997

Dear Peter,

I picked up my newspaper today to read that you were looking to ask Jürgen
'I'm on my bike' Klinsmann to be the new manager of Everton Football Club.
Forget all that stuff about them hogging the sun loungers, this guy doesn't
have his bottom on one long enough before he's eyeing up the next swimming
pool at an adjacent hotel.

Look at Spurs, run by that Essex man Alan Sugar. Would you buy a used car
from that man? Exactly, yet he sold the dream of the new tomorrow to Jürgen
when he could have been sunning it in Spain with the rest of the German nation.

When they faced you lot in the FA Cup semi-final they took a bigger bashing
than El Alemain, and Jürgen was off home to Germany because his wife was
homesick before you could say 'More deutschmarks, please'. Now he wants to
come back to England and you have his phone number.

My old dad told me 'Never trust a German who has retreated back to Bavaria',
and he knew a thing or two. In 1945 he arrested a Polish refugee with shiny
jackboots. Yeah, an SS Colonel in disguise. Wouldn't mind betting shifty
Jürgen was related to him.

Take my advice. Look no further than Mr Quips, Ron Atkinson, who needs
a stage big enough to get his roadshow back on track. He will even get the
best out of that Duncan Disorderly who plays up front for you (in between
nutting people).

Support English managers.
German divers should ply their trade in the North Sea.

William Egan

Copy to Ron Atkinson, General Manager, Coventry City

Everton
The Football Club Company Limited
Goodison Park, Liverpool L4 4EL

Mr William Egan
Guildford Road
Leatherhead
Surrey KT24 5NW

8 April 1997

Dear Mr Egan,

Thank you for your letter of 2 April 1997.

The club in the short term have appointed Dave Watson as caretaker player/manager. Our search will now start on identifying a suitable candidate to take this club into the next millennium.

The board of directors have an open mind at the moment as to the eventual manager, but recognise the need to appoint a top-quality candidate who has experience in European football.

It will come as no surprise to know that your letter is one of hundreds I have received in recent days, and you can be assured that your views and the views of all supporters are deeply respected.

Yours sincerely,

Peter R. Johnson
Chairman

Guildford Road
Leatherhead
Surrey KT24 5NW

Private and Confidential

Jürgen Klinsmann
Bayern Munich Football Club
Munich
Germany

5 April 1997

Dear Jürgen,

The tabloid newspapers in England have been hot this week with news of your imminent return to English football. What is going on? First you come to Spurs and drive around in an old battered VW, then, just as the lads have perfected their songs about you, you up sticks and return to the fatherland.

You said your wife was homesick, but surely she hasn't got over her bout of homesickness so quickly? Or has the call of the wallet got the better of you?

Culturally, you will travel to wherever the loot is the best. This is the way of all footballers, isn't it? Sounds like a good policy to me. Me and the lads work where the money is the best, so why shouldn't you? When you're out on the park give it 110 per cent, but get out the shower and start calculating where the next pay cheque comes from, eh?

Back here in Blighty (that's slang for England) the press are sharpening their knives, as they are peeved that after they voted you Footballer of the Year you returned to the land of beer and sausages.

What is the real truth behind the rumours, or do the press have to make stories up about you to fill the column inches of their newspapers?

Get back to me.

SENT SIGNED PHOTOGRAPH

William Egan

Guildford Road
Leatherhead
Surrey KT24 5NW

Dave Bassett
General Manager
Nottingham Forest Football Club
The City Ground
Nottingham NG2 5FJ

5 April 1997

Dear Fellow Cockney,

I had to write to you over a matter of national importance, namely the demise of Stuart 'Psycho' Pearce. Once upon a time he would start a run and, from fully 50 yards away, one could smell the fear in the opposing defenders. The chant would go up: 'Psycho, Psycho.' No longer. Why, you should ask yourself?

Analysis, that's what.

Now he has progressed to the upper reaches of management, he starts to think before he makes his runs. What about the space behind, etc. etc.? You know, all that fancy coaching crap.

Your prime job in life must be to get the old psycho on the move again. You know what I heard the other evening? Some wally said that the number one 'psycho' was the crazed baldy from West Ham, Julian Dicks. Quite apart from the fact that nobody called Julian could ever be deemed to be a real 'psycho', I do feel that his follically challenged appearance creates more laughter than fear.

Get back to me, as we are seriously thinking of taking Mr Psycho's name off our roll of honour.

Your psycho in the south,

William Egan

Nottingham Forest Football Club Limited
The City Ground, Nottingham NG2 5FJ

William Egan
Guildford Road
Leatherhead
Surrey KT24 5NW

16 April 1997

Dear William,

Thank you for your letter of 5 April.

As you will appreciate, Stuart Pearce has been thrust into a situation to which he is not accustomed. When Frank Clark left the club, Stuart was given management responsibilities, and things went very well at first. Then the situation took a turn for the worse. This put tremendous pressure on him – which is not surprising, bearing in mind that, in management terms, he is still a young man.

It is for this reason that I was brought into this club. My job is to help guide Stuart through this difficult period. It takes time to set up new relationships like this – and, unfortunately, time is not on our side.

It's a great pity that the takeover of the club was delayed for such a long time. When it finally went through, the club were in deep trouble and there was very little time in which to rectify the situation.

Forest will either survive in the Premiership or they will be relegated. Whatever the outcome, I have no doubt that 'Psycho' will continue to be the inspirational force behind Nottingham Forest.

Yours sincerely,

Dave Bassett
General Manager

Guildford Road
Leatherhead
Surrey KT24 5NW

Bobby Gould
Wales Manager
Welsh Football Association
3 Westgate Street
Cardiff CF1 1DD

5 April 1997

Dear Bobby,

I opened my newspaper on Wednesday to read of scandal, outrage and feud. Had Bobby Gould taken a brown envelope to throw a Wales game? No, he had passed a black bib to a black footballer and passed a justifiable comment during a match, using the phrase 'black bastard' when an opposing coloured player scored a goal after being unmarked from a corner.

So Mr Nathan Blake is offended by honest football chat? What is the world of football coming to? If an opposing player has a funny sounding name or is 6ft 5ins tall then you identify him by this characteristic, adding 'bastard' on the end if he has scored a goal against you. Your biggest mistake was not calling him a tall black bastard. And whoever was marking him must have been a blind bastard (another comment against a minority group).

Have you asked Mr Blake if he would be offended by the prefix bald, ginger, fat, ugly or Dutch? Then he gets upset because you have a joke when passing a black bib to a black footballer.

I agree with your comment that the world is a different place. Remember Henry Ford's famous comment: 'You can have any colour as long as it's black.' If some of these politically correct Johnnies had their way there would be no Ford Escorts on the road nowadays, as they'd have stopped that comment. If these jokers had been around during the war we couldn't have had a blackout, as it might have offended someone.

I remember when Bill Shankly said that you couldn't trap a bag of cement. That was unfair (but true) and a slur on an honest pro, but it was said in jest and part compliment, as Shanks never said anything about people he didn't respect. And did you cry to the newspapers? No, you laughed that famous

Bobby Gould laugh. At Wimbledon I bet you used to have black v white five-a-side matches and there was banter aplenty.

It's all got out of hand. We'll all have to chant 'black is beautiful' before breakfast at this rate. How does Nathan Blake go about his business? Did he object to you using a blackboard during team talks?

You stick to your guns, mate, and keep cracking the jokes. If Nathan can't take it in the real world he shouldn't be in football.

Call a spade a spade if that's what it is!

William Egan

The Football Association of Wales
Cymdeithas Bel Droed Cymru
Plymouth Chambers, 3 Westgate Street, Cardiff CF1 1DD

Mr William Egan
Guildford Road
Leatherhead
Surrey KT24 5NW

12 April 1997

Dear Bill,

Many things have been said over the past nine days and many things have been written, but nothing with as much conviction as your letter.

You can rest assured it will travel with me wherever I go, and to be perfectly honest, Bill, every time I look at it it will bring a smile to my face.

Kind regards.

Yours sincerely,

Bobby Gould
National Team Manager

Guildford Road
Leatherhead
Surrey KT24 5NW

Private and Confidential

Liam Brady
Youth Development Officer
Arsenal Football Club
Arsenal Stadium
Highbury
London N5 1BU

6 April 1997

Dear Liam,

I read a disturbing article in the News of the World the other Sunday. It seems that Arsène Wenger is lacing the lads' drinks with creatine, an unproved protein extract designed to give more muscle power. On top of this, all I seem to read about is the newfangled fancy pasta-with-everything diets. It seems that diet makes you play.

Correct me if I'm wrong, but weren't you 'Chippy' Brady in your heyday – and not because of your left foot's ability to ping a ball 50 yards on to a sixpence, but because of your love of chips with everything?

Spam and chips, smoked salmon and chips, and computer chips and chips were the order of the day. Didn't IBM put in a bid for you once because of your love of chips? It seemed to me that this didn't stop you being remembered as one of the all-time greats and being transferred to Italy. When you were offered the transfer to Juventus, did they ask if you liked pasta? Of course they didn't; they were more interested in whether you could play.

It would seem as if all this obsession with diet is hiding the fact that Arsenal haven't produced a half-decent player since you upped sticks for the lure of lira.

Please confirm that the emphasis at Arsenal is being placed upon skill and not on fancy diets to help players run a bit longer or extra protein so we can outmuscle Wimbledon.

A left-footer like yourself (but with a bit more malice aforethought).

William Egan

Arsenal Football Club plc
Arsenal Stadium, Highbury, London N5 IBU

Mr Egan
Guildford Road
Leatherhead
Surrey KT24 5NW

15 April 1997

Dear Mr Egan,

Thank you for your letter of 6 April – it made very interesting reading.

I want to assure you that as far as Arsène Wenger and myself are concerned, the quality of players comes first and foremost, but it will inevitably help if we can steer players in the right direction as regards diet and general awareness in what makes a career last longer.

I think Mr Wenger's choice of Patrick Vierra bears out my argument and hopefully I can prove to you in the coming years that our youth policy will produce players to your liking.

Incidentally, I love pasta but still can't go without my weekly intake of chips.

Yours sincerely,

Liam Brady
Head of Youth Development

Guildford Road
Leatherhead
Surrey KT24 5NW

Bryan Robson
Manager
Middlesbrough Football Club
Riverside Stadium
Middlesbrough TS3 6RS

6 April 1997

Dear Bryan,

I am getting worried by your policy of buying foreign players, as I have just received a message from Sir James Goldsmith saying how bad Europe is and the only logical conclusion is that the rest of the world is pretty dodgy too.

I remember you as Englishness personified: get in where it hurts, give Johnny Foreigner the retaliation first and run till the opponent cried 'ne maas' (that's 'no more' in Spanish). Now I look at you as a manager and you seem to be saying to a generation of young English guys that Johnny Foreigner can play better than us.

Are you ashamed of the way you used to kick the world and his dog over the touchline in your prime? I remember seeing you playing for West Bromwich Albion against Arsenal and you kicked the cultured Liam Brady so high he came down with snow on his head. He never recovered and you won 2–1 that day.

To make matters worse, you have a chairman who made his money selling mobile phones to English yuppies yet gives you an open invitation to move his spondulicks out to Copacabana for the retirement homes of errant Brazilians and Italians who've greyed at the edges. Did he have too much too young?

I looked at that Danish fellow called Beck playing for you. Correct me if I'm wrong, but he looks like he's got dreadlocks. Now if that isn't a mass of contradictions, then my nickname's not 'Bootsy'. As for Emerson, he hasn't been the same since he retired from active tennis and Lake and Palmer left him in the '70s.

Please confirm to me that when you have won the Coca-Cola Cup and stayed in the Premiership you are going to invest in some proper English talent in your own mould.

Your man singing 'Land of Hope and Glory',

William Egan

Middlesbrough Football Club
Cellnet Riverside Stadium, Middlesbrough TS3 6RS

William Egan
Guildford Road
Leatherhead
Surrey KT24 5NW

17 April 1997

Dear William,

Thank you for your letter to Bryan Robson which has been passed to me for reply.

Bryan thanks you for your comments, which have been noted, and sends his best wishes.

We hope we can count on your continued support of Middlesbrough Football Club.

Yours sincerely,

Diane O'Connell
Public Relations Officer

Guildford Road
Leatherhead
Surrey KT24 5NW

Ruud Gullit
Manager
Chelsea Football Club
Stamford Bridge
London SW6 1HS

6 April 1997

Dear Ruud,

You come across as more laid back than Frank Bruno when he fought Mike Tyson for the world heavyweight championship. However, I noted your comments about Eric Cantona when you were guest on BBC's *Match of the Day* last week.

All this cobblers about you playing football when all the time you are a closet Arsenal fan! Your comments about denying him space to play was straight out of the Don Howe coaching manual. Could this have anything to do with Graham Rix working as your right-hand man? Mum's the word with me (that's cockney for 'I will keep it quiet').

After all, we don't want the press giving you a hard time! You never objected when Jan Wouters used to growl around the midfield while you were stylishly floating in your prime.

Terrific stuff. Now I know that you can develop Chelsea into a force to be reckoned with. Mind you, Zola won't get as much space off those loons from Wimbledon as he got from the Spurs centre-half at Wembley when Italy played England.

However, there is a down side to all this. Being Dutch you must be a socialist, but I bet my bottom dollar that John Major tries to get a photo shoot shaking your hand between now and the general election. Don't fall for it, mate. Tell him straight in that blunt Dutch voice what you think of his politics if you don't agree.

Come on you blues.

Wembley here we come!

William Egan

Chelsea Football Club
Stamford Bridge, London SW6 1HS

W. Egan Esq.
Guildford Road
Leatherhead
Surrey KT24 5NW

19 April 1997

Dear William,

Just a short note to thank you for your very kind letter of 6 April.

By now you will be aware that we had a great result against Wimbledon
and I hope you enjoyed what was a great all-round team performance.

Many thanks for your continued support of Chelsea.

With best wishes.

Yours sincerely,

E. Gwyn Williams
Assistant Manager

Guildford Road
Leatherhead
Surrey KT24 5NW

Private and Confidential

Kenny Dalglish
Manager
Newcastle United Football Club
St James's Park
Newcastle upon Tyne NE1 4ST

6 April 1997

Dear Kenny,

I read with some discomfort that your chairman was quoted, after your 3–0 trouncing by Monaco last Wednesday, as saying that the Monaco players were fitter than the Newcastle players.

Surely there was some mistake here? I thought that fitness never came into it, although it must be remembered that these Monaco players have been brought up on a special substance diet of creatine and orange juice, which Arsène Wenger is now giving to the Arsenal players.

It doesn't matter that they will probably suffer from shrunken goolies, hair loss and high-pitched voices in later life. Let Arsène give them half a strand of extra muscle now.

Is it your view that foreign players are now fitter than English players, or is this another example of the popular press thinking up an excuse because the two best strikers in England were on the treatment table?

If foreign players are fitter, then I will have to revise my training methods for the lads' coming assault on Leatherhead Sunday League Division Eight title.

Your reply is awaited with baited breath.

William Egan

Newcastle United Football Company Limited
Registered Office: St James's Park, Newcastle upon Tyne NE1 4ST

Mr William Egan
Guildford Road
Leatherhead
Surrey KT24 5NW

10 April 1997

Dear Mr Egan,

I refer to your letter of 6 April 1997.

I cannot comment on the fitness of other players, whether they be foreign or English players. However, I can say that had both Shearer and Ferdinand been fit to play against Monaco, the outcome may have been different.

Thank you for writing to me.

Yours sincerely,

Kenny Dalglish
Team Manager

Guildford Road
Leatherhead
Surrey KT24 5NW

Peter Robinson
Chief Executive
Liverpool Football Club
Anfield Road
Liverpool L4 0TH

6 April 1997

Dear Peter,

Right on to Robbie Fowler and Steve McManaman in their support for the workers. All Liverpool players should be sporting T-shirts at the final of the Cup-Winners' Cup supporting the 500 sacked Liverpool dockers. Don't worry about Paris St Germain in the semi-final, as they all eat pasta, because they think it helps them play better, but in reality they haven't got a clue. Arsenal murdered 'em a few seasons back when Paris had a half-decent team.

I hope that Liverpool tell UEFA where to stick their sanctions and if they dare ban either of these two working-class heroes you threaten them with the European Court of Human Rights, the stocks or whatever to get them to see sense.

It's all right for the Portuguese police to open fire with machine guns on Manchester United fans in Porto, but a show of socialist solidarity is met with tough words. I'd say that the sword is more threatening than the pen in this situation. Perhaps they are frightened of losing future sponsorship money?

Please come back and confirm that Liverpool are standing four square alongside these two working-class heroes of the old school.

Support the Liverpool (dockers).

NO REPLY

William 'Bootsy' Egan

Guildford Road
Leatherhead
Surrey KT24 5NW

Lynda Lee-Potter
The Daily Mail
Northcliffe House
2 Derry Street
Kensington
London W8 5TT

6 April 1997

Dear Lynda,

May I say how much my wife enjoys your column, but who am I to be the arbiter of her taste? I'm a Daily Sport man myself – not that I buy it, but the lads who hang around all day on mindless security work have to read something to keep their minds elsewhere when sitting around while their charge endures a three-hour literary lunch.

However, despite you being a witty and incisive writer (those are my wife's words), I can't help but notice that you managed to leave out all reference to a true middle-class hero in the making. We are talking Robbie Fowler here. First-class scouse scally and Liverpool footballer, yet he allows himself time to wear a T-shirt highlighting the plight of average people working for a better future by fighting for what they believe is right.

When he scored a goal he didn't run to give the full tongue down the throat to his team-mate. No, he lifted his shirt to reveal a tasteful soliloquy about a group of workers sacked two years ago and still fighting for their jobs back – the sort of injustice you love to invoke in your column.

The absence of any comment supporting Robbie in your weekly diatribe against all that is unfair has left me baffled.

We all know the scouse jokes. How do you make a scouse omelette? First you steal three eggs! However, these guys need more than Robbie Fowler supporting them, they need stoical middle-class defenders of virtue like yourself.

Support just causes.

William Egan

The Daily Mail
Northcliffe House, 2 Derry Street, Kensington, London W8 5TT

Mr William Egan
Guildford Road
Leatherhead
Surrey KT24 5NW

17 April 1997

Dear Mr Egan,

Thank you for your letter. I am grateful you took the time and the trouble
to write to me and draw my attentions to the virtues of Robbie Fowler, and
I will certainly bear your comments in mind.

With very best wishes to you and your wife.

Yours sincerely,

Lynda Lee-Potter

Private and Confidential

Sir John Hall
Chairman
Newcastle United Football Club
St James's Park
Newcastle upon Tyne NE1 4ST

15 April 1997

Dear Sir John,

I read with some alarm that you have rescinded the banning order on the beer belly who ran on to the pitch to kiss Kevin Keegan's feet the day you beat Manchester United 5–0.

Not that I am saying that he should have been banned for wanting to kiss smelly feet; that is up to him. No, what bothers me is the fact that you did not stipulate that he dieted before he was allowed to return to watch Newcastle. In a week where you are quoted as saying that the Monaco players were fitter than the Newcastle players, you allow this man to return to watching Newcastle.

What sort of example does this set to young people, and are you condoning overweight Geordies, most of whom dream about representing Newcastle from the day they first enter one of your numerous club shops in the city?

You should threaten to ban any fans who have protruding stomachs, although from the media reports of Newcastle, Gazza and Jimmy 'Five Bellies' it would seem as if the whole of the male population of Newcastle has a belly they are proud of. It may well be that I am insulting yourself who has a 'Two Dinners' stomach (as we say in London).

Is this indeed the case and could this be the reason why Monaco were fitter than Newcastle?

I think we should be told!

<u>NO REPLY</u>

William 'Flat Belly' Egan

Guildford Road
Leatherhead
Surrey KT24 5NW

David O'Leary
Assistant Manager
Leeds United
Elland Road
Leeds
West Yorks LS11 0ES

19 April 1997

Dear David,

A disturbing new development is emerging at Highbury. It seems that Arsène Wenger (is that his real name? I can't imagine George changing his name to Leed Graham, can you?) is feeding the sturdy body of lads that you both left behind a mixture of creatine and orange juice. As if you didn't know, creatine is an unproven protein extract which might shrink Tony Adams's goolies.

This will have long-term effects on Tony, who will be deprived of his earning ability on *Match of the Day* indulging himself in comments along with Alan 'that was bad defending' Hansen. I also worry because Arsenal are now considered a good team despite having lost every big match of importance at home this season and could yet finish in the highest position since yourself and Gorgeous George left for the northern wastelands of Leeds.

What are your views on all this diet stuff? Weren't you brought up alongside Liam 'Chippy' Brady who, like Alf Tupper, tough of the track, ate fish and chips and then went out and destroyed Juventus? OK, so you were shoring up the back line most of the time, but he used to run all day without the aid of fancy diets and protein extracts. What is the world coming to? I never saw too much wrong with Arsenal's fitness when George was in charge.

Please tell me that Leeds United are not into this foreign fitness fad or dodgy foods.

Good luck next year, except when you play Arsenal.

It's all about winning.

NO REPLY

William 'Coach' Egan

Guildford Road
Leatherhead
Surrey KT24 5NW

John Giles
Football Writer
The Daily Express
Ludgate House
245 Blackfriars Road
London SE1 9UX

19 April 1997

Dear Mr Giles,

I was travelling back from Belfast a couple of days ago when a charming stewardess (wearing Manchester City colours, it might be said, although I didn't hold that against her) thrust a free copy of the Daily Express in my hand.

Turning to the back page I could find no sport. Upon turning further I came to your column. Under the axiom 'the man the players read', you opined about Middlesbrough and how Bryan Robson was manager of the year. Some manager of the year! £21 million spent and he looks like getting relegated. You also stated that Middlesbrough should reward him if he saves them this year. What with? Another £21m? In addition you described the following as a stupid question. Question from reporter after match: 'Do you think Middlesbrough will pull through?' What question should he have asked? 'Will you be drawing the job seeker's allowance if you get the gooner, Bryan?'?

I can see why some players would want to read that, as it is ambiguous enough to confuse their limited, clichéd minds. However, I would like to know how you claim that your column is read by players. In my security work all the players I meet are not intelligent enough to turn beyond the back pages, page three or the amply endowed cleavages of the Daily Sport.

Under this criteria, what statistical evidence has been compiled to suggest that you are the man the players read? Do the players get a questionnaire when they vote for their player of the year? Footballers know that sport is on the back page, so I would have to say that most footballers not only read newspapers which have sports pages in more accessible places but also read a paper which is slightly downmarket from the Daily Express.

Let me know how you came by your title, as I'm thinking of setting myself up as the man the hooligans read but don't want it challenged under the Trade Descriptions Act.

William Egan

Copy to Sports Editor, Daily Express

The Express
Ludgate House, 245 Blackfriars Road, London SE1 9UX

Mr W. Egan
Guildford Road
Leatherhead
Surrey KT24 5NW

27 April 1997

Dear Mr Egan,

Many thanks for taking the time and trouble to write to the Express, though I have to say I found your comments, while amusing, somewhat strange, to say the least.

John Giles is an intelligent, experienced commentator on the football scene whose judgement is valued highly at all levels of the game.

While he may not write the downmarket, easy-headline trash associated with the worst of the tabloids it is ludicrous to suggest that his opinions are not treated seriously by those who know what British football is about. Football is a game of opinions, and unfortunately on this occasion I happen to disagree with you.

Once again, thank you for your interest.

Yours sincerely,

Alex Butler
Head of Sport

Guildford Road
Leatherhead
Surrey KT24 5NW

Alan Fraser
Sportswriter
The Daily Mail
Northcliffe House
2 Derry Street
Kensington
London W8 5TT

19 April 1997

Dear Mr Fraser,

What are you on? Do you have psychiatric problems? I was given a free copy
of the Daily Mail last week on a flight back from working abroad to read your
article on David Elleray, the football referee of the match between
Middlesbrough and Chesterfield in the FA Cup semi-final.

The vilification that you gave him! I thought for a minute that he'd been
caught in the bushes with one of the boys he taught at Harrow School. What
did he do? He blew his whistle to deny Chesterfield a goal. A job he is
expected to do in his position. Fact: a referee seeing an infringement blows his
whistle. Just because 90 per cent of the nation wants a fairy tale to come true
and the minnows to win, it doesn't give you *carte blanche* to rubbish the man.

Your description of him as small, balding, schoolmasterly, smug, superior and
usually seen holding a red card sounds remarkably like a description of Clive
James with his arm around Margarita Prakatan (being South American she's
the red card, geddit?). Are you sure you didn't write the article while watching
his programme on Sunday evening?

In addition, you use as your expert Clive Thomas, the Welsh womble – a man
with the sobriquet 'Clive the book' when he refereed himself. It should have
given it away when Clive used the phrase 'in my day'. He was obviously
deprived of love as a child and is bigoted against today's referees, especially
Elleray. Let me remind you of Clive's finest moment. He blew his whistle one
second before the Brazilian Zico headed the winner against Sweden in the
1982 World Cup match.

Is he handpicked or what? FIFA obviously thought so, as he never officiated at the top level again. If that didn't make him bitter then nothing will.

No, sir, your article was a scandal. I hope that Elleray issues proceedings for libel, defamation of character and scandalous use of people who like sheep and live the wrong side of the River Severn.

Crusher Chits is thinking of forming the David Elleray Appreciation Society, but we won't be inviting you to the inaugural meeting.

Refereeing is an art form!

Sportswriting isn't a proper job.

William Egan

Copy to David Elleray

Guildford Road
Leatherhead
Surrey KT24 5NW

David Elleray
Football Association Referee
c/o The Football Association
16 Lancaster Gate
London W2 3LW

19 April 1997

Dear David,

I enclose a copy of the letter I have sent to Alan Fraser of the Daily Mail. Quite why you blew for that infringement when the ball was a foot over the line only you know, but the fact of the matter is that too many amateur referees are writing articles nowadays.

As a referee myself I know the pressures you are under. The difference between me and you, though, is the fact that I can slap the nut on recalcitrant players, as the leagues I operate in have no rules except that he who's toughest survives.

Keep whistling and keep out of the bushes in case I have given the press another way of defaming you.

Are you interested in our David Elleray Appreciation Society?

Referees do it with whistles!

William 'Bootsy' Egan

Harrow

25 April 1997

Dear Bill,

Many thanks for being a vocal source of support to referees. If there were more like you, referees might get a fairer hearing.

Best wishes,

David Elleray

Guildford Road
Leatherhead
Surrey KT24 5NW

Alan Fraser
Sportswriter
The Daily Mail
Northcliffe House
2 Derry Street
Kensington
London W8 5TT

1 May 1997

Dear Mr Fraser,

I have received no reply to my factually based argument of 19 April regarding Mr David Elleray, referee of the year and decent chap all round. When did you last read of a referee fiddling his expense account or falling over tired and emotional?

Crusher Chits has now formed the David Elleray Appreciation Society. One of his first acts is to take some unfortunate hack to task over the calumnies they spread about honest people. Looking at your track record, it could well be you.

I await your reply.

Referees do it with a whistle.

Support the man in black.

Sportswriting isn't a proper job.

William Egan

Copies to: Ian Wooldridge, sportswriter
            Brian Scovell, cricket correspondent

The Daily Mail
Northcliffe House, 2 Derry Street, Kensington, London W8 5TT

Mr William Egan
Guildford Road
Leatherhead
Surrey KT24 5NW

7 May 1997

Dear Bill,

And I thought this was an exclusive letter to me. It seems you are writing to any Tom, Dick, Wooldridge and Scovell.

Sportswriters do it on a Tandy.

Yours sincerely,

Alan Fraser
Sports Feature Writer

Guildford Road
Leatherhead
Surrey KT24 5NW

Baddiel
Football Columnist
The Mirror
Holborn Circus
London EC1P 1DQ

19 April 1997

Bad Bad Baddiel,

In a world where good is bad and bad is about as good as it gets, I have to point out to you that your article in the Mirror on 22 March 1997 overstepped the bounds of taste within the current football climate.

We live in a world where passing black bibs to Welsh footballers is deemed unacceptable. (Thank God he didn't get a sheepskin one, as that would really have upset a Welshman.) You then insult one Iain Dowie by calling him ugly. Just because you are no oil painting yourself!

Pardon me, mate, but how do you think Iain feels? Give Nathan Blake a black bib and dare to prefix 'bastard' with 'black', and the world and his dog are up in arms saying that racism must be cut out of football. Call someone ugly and it's OK. Not where I come from it ain't. If you had called Paul Ince 'Sambo' you'd be looking at a racism charge, but you get away with calling an Irishman ugly.

To make it worse you start going on about how wonderful-looking a Portuguese Mr Dani is, and how he scores great goals against Austrian no-hopers. Well, unless you've had your head up your bottom, mate, it won't have escaped your notice that even Frank Skinner could score against Austrians. Scotsmen, in the form of Kevin Gallagher, score great goals against Austrians because their football is crap and they eat sausages.

All you did was write a song. Bernard Manning cracks jokes about black people and is ostracised, yet I haven't seen one person saying that you should be barred from football grounds for calling Iain Dowie ugly. I bet he'd rip that curtain ring out of your ear if he got hold of you.

NO REPLY

William Egan

146

Guildford Road
Leatherhead
Surrey KT24 5NW

The Sports Editor
The Mirror
Holborn Circus
London EC1P 1DQ

19 April 1997

Dear Sir,

I was brought up in a house where even the cat was a Tory. So you can imagine the horror of my father when I started to read the Mirror. Mind you, that was when it was the Daily Mirror, a paper with standards.

So imagine my shock when I read the following comment by Baddiel: 'That just means that some ugly bloke somewhere has been deprived of a talent for the game that should have been his (Iain Dowie, if you're reading this, I don't mean you).' Not only do you employ people who don't have a Christian name, but you also allow gratuitous comments about ugly people.

I note that you seem to be running a campaign against Terry Venables acting correctly within the law, yet allow this sort of racism. Don't get me wrong; I've punched a few ugly mugs in my time (along with a few pretty ones), but we live in a different era. Imagine if everybody started chanting 'Iain, you are ugly' at the next West Ham away match. How would his wife and children feel?

Humour is OK when done in the right place; personal abuse regarding ugliness is not and is below the belt.

I await your explanation for this disgusting journalistic lapse in taste and confirmation that the writer with no Christian name who was responsible, Baddiel, will not be writing for the Mirror again.

William Egan

Copies to: Roy Hattersley MP, football writer
            David Lacey, Sportswriter of the Year

Letter sent demanding personal explanation.

Guildford Road
Leatherhead
Surrey KT24 5NW

The Sports Editor
The Mirror
Holborn Circus
London EC1P 1DQ

9 May 1997

Dear Sir,

I have received no reply to my letter dated 19 April regarding the disgraceful comments made by one of your columnists, Mr Baddiel.

I am in central London next week along with Crusher Chits and Strace. Perhaps we should pop in for a friendly chat about the depths your paper is sinking to by calling Iain Dowie ugly.

Shall we say about 4.30 p.m. next Thursday?

William Egan

The Mirror
One Canada Square, Canary Wharf, London E14 5AP

William Egan
Guildford Road
Leatherhead
Surrey KT24 5NW

14 May 1997

Dear Mr Egan,

Thank you for your letter dated 9 May. Our offices moved to Canada Square, Canary Wharf, three years ago, and I can only assume that your letter dated 19 April has not been forwarded to our new headquarters.

I am sorry, but I have other commitments next Thursday and will not be able to meet you. However, as we are no longer based in central London it is probably not convenient for you either.

Yours sincerely

David Balmforth
Sports Editor

Guildford Road
Leatherhead
Surrey KT24 5NW

Ken Bates
Chairman
Chelsea Football Club
Stamford Bridge
London SW6 1HS

19 April 1997

Dear Ken,

What a result. Artistes 3, Artisans 0. Never in doubt from the moment the
sun shone on the Italian backs. They could have been on the Italian Riviera
instead of at Highbury. However, I was a bit disturbed by the number of
Chelsea fans who took their shirts off to reveal large expanses of beer belly.
That is something Geordies do. It isn't the Chelsea way. I hope you advise
against this behaviour at Wembley or else quality foreign players may be put
off signing for Chelsea in the future.

Now we're at the twin towers you need a record to gee things along and have
I got the cup final record for the boys! Remember the 1975 record 'Do the
Hustle' from Van McCoy and the Soul City Symphony? Well, how about
Chelsea doing this but changing the words to 'do the Zola'? This will kill two
birds with one stone, as one can't expect the foreign lads to sing along to the
usual bland lyrics. As the only lyric in the song is 'do the hustle', the players
can all shout 'do the Zola' in unison without embarrassing the foreign lads.

Whilst the instrumental plays, the lads can 'do the Zola' in the background –
which could revolve around the aeroplane movement Zola currently uses. I
can recommend the dance done in and around Bookham by the Chelsea lads
which is a derivative of the 'Tanner'. This was a dance perfected to this record
by Des 'Two Breakfasts' Tanner, in which he moved his considerable belly
forward while moving the arms back and vice versa. Loads of enthusiasm but
no style. Rather like Wimbledon, don't you think!

As none of the lads has the belly for this, I can recommend Beamus Gallagher,
Mad Dog Johnston and Steve the Landlord as background dancers whose
gaits are well equipped for such a performance. I also have an idea for a
double A side featuring a rewrite of 'Everybody Wants to Be a Cat',

substituting 'blue' for 'cat'. I am available for all rewrites and choreography in return for a seat in the royal box, as long as I don't have to sit next to John Major. I can't stand to see a grown man cry. It will be 1 May, not cup final day, which will see the only blues defeat in London.

However, I won't be offended if you just want my musical talents and leave the royal box duties to yourself, David Mellor and Ossie Osgood.

Get back to me early, as I'm nearly fully booked for May and I want to ensure that the Italian contingent really feel at home with their own cup final record.

Come on you blues.

Your man in blue,

William Egan

Copy to Eric 'Monster' Hall, football agent

Chelsea Football Club
Stamford Bridge, London SW6 1HS

Mr W. Egan
Guildford Road
Leatherhead
Surrey KT24 5NW

22 April 1997

Dear Mr Egan,

Thank you for your letter dated 19 April 1997 and your suggestion for a cup final record. Unfortunately your letter arrived yesterday, two days after the team recorded a cup final song!

Yours sincerely,

Ken Bates
Chairman

Guildford Road
Leatherhead
Surrey KT24 5NW

Tony Blair
Leader
New Labour Party
150 Walworth Road
London SE17 1JJ

25 April 1997

Dear Fellow New Man,

For the past few weeks I have been writing to your top men to tell them that you would lose the election if you didn't get on the football bandwagon, as no 'New Labour' politician worth his flat cap could afford to miss out on the football ticket, which is big business and media-friendly at the current time.

I noted how the Tory mob had suddenly become attending Chelsea fans and not the closet ones who only watch it on Sky TV. They are all there with their 'I don't take bribes' grins. I doubt it is lost on you that Chelsea (the blues) are having rather a good time of it at the moment, and are sort of rising from the dead, so to speak. Chelsea actually win a couple of matches and John Boy calls a snap election. Coincidence? Perhaps not!

Then, after seemingly ignoring my exhortations, you slipped down the opinion polls faster than a sad Tory slips a brown envelope in his pocket. So, stone the crows if I don't switch on my telly last night to see you kicking a ball around, Nelson Mandela style. Result? A rise of ten points in the polls immediately. Ignore the football ticket at your peril, eh?

I'll get back to you after the election when you've got the carpet slippers on in front of the No. 10 fire. One word of caution, though, mate. That tracksuit looked a little dodgy, so here's a fiver to help you invest in a new one. However, it must go on a new tracksuit. I don't want you to spend it investing in some one-parent dykes' club in Islington.

Come on you reds.

William Egan

NO REPLY

Enc. £5 note

152

Guildford Road
Leatherhead
Surrey KT24 5NW

Patrick Collins
Chief Sportswriter
The Mail on Sunday
Northcliffe House
2 Derry Street
Kensington
London W8 5TT

26 April 1997

Dear Patrick,

Nice article on Sebastian Coe the other Sunday. Funny how you managed to write an article about athletics and mention Seb electioneering in Cornwall at the same time. Nice coincidence, that. Are you a fully paid-up member of his re-election team?

If you're going to support the man, why didn't you just write the following: As Sebastian Coe glided around the bend of the Los Angeles Coliseum for his second 1,500 metres gold medal, he realised that it was Conservative sports policies which had made it all possible. Trailing in his wake were two Labour supporters, Cram and Ovett.

However, I fail to see why Seb was moaning about the new breed of athletes who are more concerned about their appearance money and perks. Wasn't it Maggie Thatcher who stated that there is no such thing as communities, only individuals? I don't see too many of her mob not getting their snouts into the trough when it's necessary (and that's most of the time).

No, you could have written a glorious piece on working-class hero Robbie Fowler or a piece condemning the machine-gun-wielding Portuguese cops attacking innocent Manchester United fans (pity they didn't get old sour-face Ferguson himself with a stray bullet), but you chose good old Tory Sebastian Coe! Is there something we should be told? Do you have shares in his health clubs?

I await your reply.

William Egan

The Mail on Sunday
Northcliffe House, 2 Derry Street, Kensington, London W8 5TT

William Egan Esq.
Guildford Road
Leatherhead
Surrey KT24 5NW

30 April 1997

Dear Mr Egan,

Thank you for your letter concerning my recent article on Seb Coe. I receive hundreds of letters every year, but I don't think I have ever been so totally misunderstood.

You seem to find it sinister that Coe should appear in my column at a time when he was seeking re-election. But that was the reason for writing the column. One of the most celebrated sportsmen of the century is, it seems highly likely, about to close an important chapter of his life. It was a compelling theme for an article, and the Observer clearly thought the same way, since they published a similar piece on the same day.

I have known Coe very well for many years, and I know that he would find the notion of my joining his re-election team quite hilarious. As for writing a piece supporting the 'working-class hero Robbie Fowler', well, I did. In the Mail on Sunday on 30 March. You really should have read it.

Finally, you mentioned the 'Labour supporter' Steve Ovett. By coincidence, he is another good friend of mine. In fact, during last year's Atlanta Olympics, I had a £10 bet with him on the likely outcome of the British general election. As you will see from the date on this letter, I am writing this on the day before the poll, and the outcome is obviously unknown. But I can tell you that I backed the Labour Party . . . and I fully expect to collect.

Yours sincerely,

Patrick Collins

Guildford Road
Leatherhead
Surrey KT24 5NW

Private and Confidential

Sepp Blatter
General Secretary FIFA
PO Box 85
Hitzigweg 11
8030 Zurich
Switzerland

26 April 1997

Dear Sepp,

It is an Englishman's right to watch football in every country in the world. I
feel that this should be written in the front of every Englishman's passport
(forget the Scots, Welsh and Irish, as we are the chosen people).

However, your recent actions have made it difficult for an Englishman to sail
away from the white cliffs of Dover without worrying about how Johnny
Foreigner will react when he sees a full-blooded English football fan drinking
on foreign soil.

Firstly, I am confused and outraged all at the same time. Robbie Fowler bares
his chest to reveal support for working-class heroes (Liverpool dockers) and you
fine him instead of giving him a medal. Then a few days later you send a letter
of congratulation because he shows the same sense of fair play during a match
against Arsenal, when he tells the referee the truth.

Forgive me, as I'm no 'two brains', but weren't both actions the same? Tell it
like it is and prevent injustice. Please explain that to me.

Then, to compound all these mistakes, I read about the innocent Manchester
United fans getting machine-gunned in Portugal just because Man U won
4–0. I scanned the papers waiting for a strongly worded condemnation from
FIFA of the fascist bully boys, but what do I read? Absolutely nothing.

Does FIFA operate a different policy for English football fans from that used
for the rest of the world? I have recently written to our Foreign Secretary,
asking about the attitude of the Italian police for the forthcoming World Cup

qualifying match. The last time we were there the Italian police chartered an airliner and deported the first 342 English fans they could arrest (funny how that was the exact number of seats on the plane). They are not answering. Sinister, don't you think?

See what you can find out. I enclose 20 francs to help pay for your return postage, as I understand that this is the way things are done at FIFA.

Bring the World Cup home to England in 2004.

Yours sincerely,

William Egan

Enc. 20 French francs

FIFA
For the Good of the Game
Fédération Internationale de Football Association
PO Box 85, Hitzigweg 11, 8030 Zurich, Switzerland

Mr William Egan
Guildford Road
Leatherhead
Surrey KT24 5NW
England

5 May 1997

Dear Mr Egan,

Thank you for your letter of 26 April to the General Secretary.

It is indeed the right of everybody to watch football anywhere in the world, not just of the English! But you appear to be confused with regard to the two incidents concerning Robbie Fowler. While it was indeed FIFA who wrote a letter of congratulation for Fowler's display of fair play against Arsenal, it was UEFA who fined him for his display of solidarity with the Liverpool dockers, as this incident occurred in a UEFA competition.

Similarly, the incidents at the Porto v Manchester United match were a UEFA matter, and in the meantime UEFA have imposed a heavy fine and other measures on Porto.

With regard to the England v Italy match later this year, you may be assured that the Italian authorities will do what is necessary to ensure that the match goes ahead as football-loving fans would wish it to. This of course also requires both sets of fans to play their part.

Regarding your wish to 'bring the World Cup home to England in 2004', we assume you mean 2006. There we shall have to wait and see.

I enclose your 20 franc note; maybe you would like to donate it to our adopted charity, SOS Children's Villages, or a similar organisation, as this is 'the way things are done in FIFA'.

Yours sincerely,

Keith Cooper
Director of Communications

Guildford Road
Leatherhead
Surrey KT24 5NW

Private and Confidential

Lennart Johansson
General Secretary UEFA
Chemin de la Redoute 54
CH-1260 Nyon 2
Switzerland

26 April 1997

Dear Lennart,

I am very worried by the actions of Sepp Blatter, who I believe does not have the Swedish sense of fair play and so will be favouring the German bid for the 2006 World Cup.

His actions have made it very difficult for an Englishman to sail away from the white cliffs of Dover without worrying about how Johnny Foreigner will react when he sees a full-blooded English football fan drinking on foreign soil.

Firstly, I am confused and outraged all at the same time. Robbie Fowler bares his chest to reveal support for working-class heroes (Liverpool dockers) and FIFA fine him instead of giving him a medal. Then a few days later they send a letter of congratulation because he shows the same sense of fair play during a match against Arsenal, when he tells the referee the truth.

Forgive me, as I'm no 'two brains', but weren't both actions the same? Tell it like it is and prevent injustice. Please explain that to me.

Then, to compound all these mistakes, I read about the innocent Manchester United fans getting machine-gunned in Portugal just because Man U won 4–0. I scanned the papers waiting for a strongly worded condemnation from FIFA of the fascist bully boys, but what do I read? Absolutely nothing.

Does FIFA operate a different policy for English football fans from that in use for the rest of the world? If they do, then this will have a bearing on England's bid for the 2006 World Cup. I have also just read that a Swiss referee has been banned for accepting bribes. This is on top of the man Tapie buying Marseilles the European Cup win. Is this sort of thing rife over there? Being an island race we don't know about the form. Does England need to dish out a few brown envelopes to get the nod? If they do, I can write to John Major, who is about to get voted out. He's pretty laid back about such things, as his ministers are at it regularly.

Anyway, get back to me, as my election advice about football has been taken up by all the main parties so I will probably be asked to help plan the strategy of the bid for the 2006 World Cup. We can't give it to the Germans again after our tremendous performance in Euro 96.

How many songs do the Germans write about football which get a whole nation singing? Come to think of it, I can't think of one German pop group.

I enclose 10 Dutch guilders for return postage.

Bring the World Cup home to England in 2006.

Yours sincerely,

William Egan

Enc. 10 Dutch guilders

Private and Confidential

Lennart Johansson
General Secretary UEFA
Chemin de la Redoute 54
CH-1260 Nyon 2
Switzerland

9 May 1997

Dear Lennart,

Not only am I worried about Sepp Blatter's sense of fair play, but I am also worried about yours. I sent you a letter recently containing some money to help smooth things along (the UEFA way), but I have received no reply. Could it be one of the chaps (or chapesses) has put it forward into their red-light-district fund? I have read that referees in Italy have nice young nubile ladies who act as interpreters but also double up with relief massage.

I thought you were Swedish and so insisted on fair play and equality within the law to play Abba records and drive Volvos to the sauna. Mind you, liberal minded you may be, but what about the price of lager? Mad Monty had to take out a second mortgage when he bought a round in Stockholm.

Get back to me on this as I have advised the English FA to start negative campaigning. Obviously, evidence of dastardly deeds like intercepting mail and stuffing bank notes into the back pocket will be sound stuff to start with. That sort of thing has just cost the Conservatives their meal ticket, so I know how to make this work. I also understand that you favour the English option for the World Cup bid, as you've had a couple of tête-à-têtes with John Major since Euro 96.

I enclose 1,000 Spanish pesetas for return postage.

Bring the World Cup home to England in 2006.

William Egan

Enc. 1,000 Spanish pesetas

UEFA
Union des associations européennes de football
Chemin de la Redoute 54, CH-1260 Nyon 2

Mr William Egan
Guildford Road
Leatherhead
Surrey KT24 5NW
United Kingdom

16 May 1997

Dear Sir,

On behalf of the UEFA president, Mr Lennart Johansson, we thank you for your letters of 26 April and 9 May 1997 and we have taken note of their contents.

We return the 1,000 Spanish pesetas and the 10 Dutch guilders to you.

Yours faithfully

U.R. Rothenbühler
Attaché to the Presidium

Guildford Road
Leatherhead
Surrey KT24 5NW

Brian Glanville
Chief Football Correspondent
The Times
1 Pennington Street
London E1 9XN

26 April 1997

Dear Brian,

I couldn't help but notice how tired you looked on the picture they use in the paper. Like a war correspondent who has been at the front for too long. Unfortunately, in your piece about the Middlesbrough v Chesterfield match, for the first time you started to write like one.

Instead of writing about the power of English football and the joyous expression of the British love of an underdog following the humiliation of the cream of world football representing Middlesbrough in the FA Cup semi-final, you harped on about the lack of expression from Middlesbrough. Don't you realise that the closest some of those Chesterfield players have got to Brazil before that semi-final was a jar of Nescafé?

Chesterfield summed up everything that Mad Monty, Crusher Chits and myself represent when we tour on foreign soil following Arsenal and England. Meanwhile, old tired-eyes sees no respite from the doom and gloom. Can life really be that gloomy from the press box?

Take a holiday and chill out for a few weeks. You'll have plenty of chances to give England a hard time when they play away in Poland and Italy. Oh for the glory days of Desmond Hackett of the Daily Express, when every football match was graphically reproduced like a combination of Dunkirk, with Stukas screaming in, and an *Eastenders* day out in Margate.

Yours sincerely,

William Egan

The Times
1 Pennington Street, London E1 9XN

13 May 1997

Dear Mr Egan,

What a bizarre letter. I am not the Football Correspondent of The Times, nor did I cover Middlesbrough v Chesterfield.

Perhaps it is you who should take a holiday.

Yours truly,

Brian Glanville

Guildford Road
Leatherhead
Surrey KT24 5NW

Craig Brown
Manager, Scotland Football Team
Scottish Football Association
6 Park Gardens
Glasgow G3 7YE

26 April 1997

Dear Craig,

As an Englishman and proud I am honour bound to point out to you the bias being shown to Scotland during World Cup qualifying campaigns. Is it my imagination or do Scotland seem to constantly get easy qualifying groups?

Look at this time. We get Italy, Poland and Georgia. Scotland get Austria, Sweden and Estonia. I won't even mention Belarus, as that sounds like a scary ride in Euro Disney. I just can't imagine a song 'Belarus on My Mind'. Can you?

Not satisfied with an easy ride to France 98, you try and make it difficult by not even scoring in Estonia when the other team don't turn up. What do they teach footballers in training? Always finish. So, against Estonia in Tallin (isn't that the black stuff in tea?) you kick off – lucky you never lost the toss – and then the boys immediately throw their arms up in celebration. Result? FIFA declares the match a draw. Now if young Jocky had run down the pitch and rifled the ball into an empty onion bag you'd have been 1–0 up and FIFA couldn't have declared the match a draw and ordered a replay.

Me and the lads reckon that your qualification path is eased by those politically correct foreigners at FIFA who are egged on by the sportswriting fraternity led by Hugh McIlvanney and Patrick Barclay.

William Egan

Copy to Ian Wooldridge, Daily Mail

Patron: Her Majesty The Queen
The Scottish Football Association
6 Park Gardens, Glasgow G3 7YE

William Egan Esq.
Guildford Road
Leatherhead
Surrey KT24 5NW

13 May 1997

Dear Mr Egan,

While England played a series of friendly matches to qualify for Euro 96 we had ten demanding qualification games!

I would contend that Austria and Sweden represent stiffer opposition than Poland and Georgia. Stiffer by a mile! Anyway, I wish to point out that our qualification path is anything but easy and that, as always, we shall do our best to make it to France in 1998.

It is a fact I assume everyone would agree with that Italy are an outstanding team, but that apart I don't see much opposition to England in their group.

It is significant that major papers have Scotsmen as major writers. Messrs McIlvanney and Barclay are superb exponents, as are Messrs Ferguson and Graham in the Premiership!

Thank you for your controversial letter; hence the controversial reply!

Yours sincerely,

Craig Brown
International Team Manager

Guildford Road
Leatherhead
Surrey KT24 5NW

Patrick Barclay
Chief Football Correspondent
The Sunday Telegraph
Peterborough Court at South Quay
181 Marsh Wall
London E14 9SR

26 April 1997

Dear Mr Barclay,

I refuse to call you a bald bastard, which you asked me to do in your letter dated 3 March 1997, as I consider that tabloid speak. There are many follically challenged men who are very successful. Clive James springs to mind, along with the rug traders Paul Daniels and Bruce Forsyth. However, your self-deprecation about your bonce isn't the reason for writing.

I would like to take you up on your offer of a drink and a discussion and I will buy you a beer, although seeing as your expense account is substantially larger than mine, on my round I'll drink cheap stuff and on yours it's designer lager.

Not that I'm sure that Poland sells designer beers, but I'm out there working the week of the England match so I'll meet you at your hotel early Friday evening. I have a business proposition to discuss with you, as my newly earned diploma in creative writing has earned me the chance to write and get paid. Nice work if you can get it. Watch out, mate, because not only can I write, I've also got a full head of hair.

Get back to me with a phone number so we can set this up.

We'll spoof for the first round.

William Egan

The Sunday Telegraph
1 Canada Square, Canary Wharf, London E14 5AR

7 May 1997

Dear Bill,

Thanks for your letter. It wasn't self-deprecation about my bonce. Baldness is no more a fault than being black. It's not a disability either, although most haired people seem to think so.

By all means come to the hotel in Poland before the England match and we'll have a few beers. Call me on the office number.

Best wishes,

Patrick

Guildford Road
Leatherhead
Surrey KT24 5NW

Christopher Martin-Jenkins
c/o The Daily Telegraph
Peterborough Court at South Quay
181 Marsh Wall
London E14 9SR

26 April 1997

Fellow Cricket Fan,

Travelling back from a continental soirée recently I read with alarm your article on the England cricket team. In a week when the Aussie Mark Waugh has started a war of words over the forthcoming Ashes series, I feel I have the answer to England's cricket problems.

I noted your comments about England's cricketers being roundly condemned at cricket dinners the length and breadth of the country. As a football man, I believe that this is the root cause of the problem. At these dinners who was there to defend himself? If that had been football there would have been uproar, with bread rolls and fisticuffs everywhere.

That's the problem, mate. No passion. Do you think that England's footballers would allow themselves to be roundly condemned at football dinners? No, they'd have been there drinking the free booze and getting outside early for a knee-trembler with a pretty waitress.

Then the press have a field day, so the lads all make a commitment to stick together. Result? Stronger *esprit de corps*. What is cricket's answer? To send them on a course to play mind games with Will Carling, a rugby player who shit his pants when confronted by a big mean Kiwi called Jonah Lomu. What an example to the boys who will have to face the sledging tactics of those crims from down under! Use your column to tell cricket to get mean via the football route.

I await your reply on this matter.

Yours sincerely,

William Egan

The Daily Telegraph
1 Canada Square, Canary Wharf, London E14 5DT

Bill Egan Esq.
Guildford Road
Leatherhead
Surrey KT24 5NW

11 June 1997

Dear Bill,

Thank you for your letter and many apologies for the long-delayed response.

I agree with you, I think!

I am forever advocating passion in our cricket team, so long as it is controlled.

At Edgbaston it was and long may it continue.

Yours sincerely,

Christopher Martin-Jenkins

Guildford Road
Leatherhead
Surrey KT24 5NW
England

Nelson Mandela
President
Republic of South Africa
Parliament Street
Cape Town
South Africa

1 May 1997

Honourable Leader,

We were reading about you the other day and the fact of the matter is, mate, that you've done more porridge (time in prison) than Strace the Ace. Not that it's done you any harm. After all, you are the top man now, with free entry into all sporting events (and don't you take advantage of that). Strace, in the meantime, finds himself banned from most English football grounds, but he's not a bitter man, so do not lose any sleep or start a world campaign.

No, the reason we are writing is that we have had a bet. We reckon you were a footy wizard in your youth and I was wondering if you'd settle our wager.

I reckon you were a tough, uncompromising centre-half, whereas Chits reckons you were a bit of a tricky left-winger type.

Please confirm this, and I wonder if you'd provide a signed photo for the chaps, as we'd like to auction it at our yellow paint Shed reunion dinner.

Look forward to hearing from you.

William Egan

Office of the President
Tuynhuys, Private Bag X1000, Cape Town 8000

Mr William Egan
Guildford Road
Leatherhead
Surrey KT24 5NW
England

16 May 1997

Dear Mr Egan,

Thank you for your letter of 1 May 1997. President Mandela was never a 'footy wizard' in his youth. Consequently he was not a 'tricky left-winger type'. We assume that 'footy' means football, or soccer.

We are sorry that someone had to lose a wager.

With kind regards,

A.M. Kathrada
Parliamentary Counsellor in the Office of the President

Guildford Road
Leatherhead
Surrey KT24 5NW

Jane Moore
Sun Woman Editor
The Sun
1 Virginia Street
London E1 9XP

1 May 1997

Dear Jane,

Don't get me wrong; I'm no misogynist – I find Jo Brand's jokes about men funny (does that make me queer?) – but your article about Matt le Tissier, England footballer, leaving his wife for a younger model is wider than an Eric Cantona shot against Borussia Dortmund.

Footballers don't have anything different that makes them want to score extra marital, it's just that as soon as a woman finds out a young man is a footballer she's got her knickers in her handbag faster than a Conservative politician can stuff the brown envelope in the back pocket.

Look at the only woman in power in football: Karen Brady. She stated that she didn't fancy footballers because all they were worried about was the size of their willies. Ten minutes later she's married one and has a sprog in her arms.

The truth of the matter is that women throw themselves at footballers and unless the young man is a raving poofter or is having bromide in his early-morning tea (as happens presently at Arsenal under Arsène Wenger), it's blooming difficult for them to stop playing away.

Closer to the point is the fact that you have probably thrown yourself at a few footballers in your time – which has obviously and sadly long since past – but they snubbed you.

William 'Ex-Footballer' Egan

The Sun
1 Virginia Street, London E1 9XP

Bill Egan
Guildford Road
Leatherhead
Surrey KT24 5NW

Date as Postmark

Dear Mr Egan,

Thank you for taking the time to write to me with your comments. I read your letter with interest.

I do hope that you continue to read and enjoy the Sun.

Yours sincerely,

Jane Moore
Woman's Editor

Guildford Road
Leatherhead
Surrey KT24 5NW

Peter Reid
Manager
Sunderland Football Club
Roker Park
Sunderland SR6 9SW

1 May 1997

Dear Peter,

Almost at the end of a long, hard season. Whether or not you stay up is irrelevant, as nobody could accuse you of not giving it your best shot. Goals are the name of the game, and that's the department in which you're sadly lacking. Mind you, where can you find centre-forwards nowadays? A bad one is quoted at £5 million. How much would your old mate Andy Gray be worth now? Especially now he can paint the TV screen while he talks on Sky TV.

I'm not in the advice game, as there are thousands of Wearsiders giving you that every week, but I do feel that you need to make sure that next year everybody feels at home in your new stadium. Your unsmiling boat (boat race: face) is worrying to young children and adults alike, so to ensure that everybody feels good in the new stadium and that they don't catch your worry vibes, I suggest you get in one of these Feng Shui consultants. For those not in the know, it is the ancient art of furniture arrangement. Make sure the seats are bolted down in the right place. All the top bods are having it done in London. One can't open a restaurant without inviting a Feng Shui specialist.

Mind you, a word of caution. Alan Sugar got one in at Spurs and she recommended they turn the seats away from the pitch. Not a bad judge, eh?

I recommend that you get the lads to chant this before your last matches. It should help to relieve the tension: 'Win or lose, we'll have a booze. If we draw we'll have some more!'

William Egan

Sunderland AFC
The Caring Club
Roker Park, Sunderland SR6 9SW

Mr W. Egan
Guildford Road
Leatherhead
Surrey KT24 5NW

7 May 1997

Dear Egan,

Thank you for your letter. Your support and best wishes are very much appreciated. I shall bear in mind the Feng Shui consultants!

With kind regards.

Yours sincerely,

Peter Reid
Manager

Guildford Road
Leatherhead
Surrey KT24 5NW

Private and Confidential

Elton John
Owner, Watford Football Club Ltd
Vicarage Road Stadium
Watford WD1 8ER

4 May 1997

Dear Elton,

So the week that Elton makes his comeback to Watford, Tony Blair gets elected to No. 10. Are the two events related, by any chance? I would like to think so. What you need is to get the team sorted out, so the first thing you need to do is get Graham Taylor out of the board room and back into a tracksuit. He should have got over his disappointment at being sacked by England and Watford need his inspiration to get out of that lowly division.

My earliest memories of Watford are all fond, coming up there and seeing the little space invader men on the electronic scoreboard jump up and down when Watford scored. Inspirational stuff – but quite funny for a travelling Arsenal supporter.

That is where I see your role. Inspirational. Use your ability to write some stirring music that the team can run out to. Those boys need to feel that they are ten feet tall. Whatever else Watford have, they should have the best sound system and musical accompaniment with a famous pop star as owner. Everybody's at the music wheeze nowadays, so how about you using your talents to write something punchy and catchy, like the old 'Saturday Night's All Right for Watford' sort of thing? If you can insert the lyrics 'Do I not like that' then so much the better. After all, the bitch is back, eh?

Welcome Home (Peters and Lee)

William Egan

Watford
Registered Office and Ground: Watford Association Football Club Ltd
Vicarage Road Stadium, Watford WD1 8ER

Mr W. Egan
Guildford Road
Leatherhead
Surrey KT24 5NW

22 May 1997

Dear Bill,

Would you believe that your letter dated 4 May addressed to Elton John by some coincidence arrived in my mail already opened?

I have of course passed it on to Elton, but I thought I would take this opportunity of replying to you.

I am a 52-year-old grandfather – not a 32-year-old 'whipper snapper' from Lincoln – but I feel just as excited about putting the tracksuit back on as I did when I first joined Watford in 1977.

Hopefully, that does answer your question about getting over the disappointment of being 'sacked by England'. Actually I resigned, would you believe, because the Football Association were reluctant to sack me! In other words, I forced them to kick me out! Although in all truthfulness I do not think they needed all that much forcing!

Let's look forward to the future, and hopefully this is the start of another successful era for Watford and all of the club's supporters.

Best wishes,

Graham Taylor

Guildford Road
Leatherhead
Surrey KT24 5NW

Martin Edwards
Chief Executive
Manchester United Football Club
Sir Matt Busby Way
Old Trafford
Manchester M16 0RA

4 May 1997

Dear Martin,

Do I not like the rubbish that has been written about Manchester United over the past couple of weeks? What have you done to deserve this vilification? Earning too much money, that's all. So you lost a European Cup semi-final after dominating both legs.

If we look at the facts, we see that Dortmund had three shots over two matches and scored two goals, while you scored none after peppering their goal with numerous shots which hit the post, bar and that lucky German bastard's legs when he was down and out. In Dortmund the Germans breathed such a huge sigh of relief that it could be heard as far away as the towel-draped sunbeds in Tenerife. Not only that, but not one of the sportswriters predicted anything other than a Manchester victory before the match, yet after the final whistle the Captain Hindsights were amazing in their ability to condemn even the Coronation Street cat. As for the 'get rid of Cantona' cant, it's a worrying trend. However, as most sportswriters have difficulty seeing beyond the end of their noses due to their nocturnal habits (sends them blind), it is not something you should be taking too much notice of.

For this reason I am sending you 10 deutschmarks so that you can forward it to the sportswriter who you feel excelled in the anti-Man U rhetoric. This will help pay for the huge amounts of beer he obviously drank in the beer capital of Germany, so rendering his one remaining brain cell worthless.

Get back to me and let me know who you made the recipient of this.

Tony Blair's a gooner! (That's an Arsenal fan; he lives in Islington.)

William Egan
Enc. 10 deutschmarks

The Manchester United Football Club plc
Sir Matt Busby Way, Old Trafford, Manchester M16 0RA

Mr W. Egan
Guildford Road
Leatherhead
Surrey KT24 5NW

6 May 1997

Dear Mr Egan,

Thank you for taking the time and trouble to write such a supportive letter.

I do not feel, however, that it would be appropriate to forward the 10 deutschmarks to any of the sportswriters who have been criticising Manchester United over the past few weeks and I am, therefore, returning the note to you.

Kind regards.

Yours sincerely,

C. Martin Edwards
Chairman

Guildford Road
Leatherhead
Surrey KT24 5NW

Brian Scovell
Sportswriter
The Daily Mail
Northcliffe House
2 Derry Street
Kensington
London W8 5TT

4 May 1997

Dear Brian,

I'm a worried Pom after reading your article on the 19 players purporting to represent the English cricket team retreating into rural Oxfordshire to play mind games to toughen them up for the forthcoming Ashes series against the roughest, toughest Aussie team ever to visit this island since a boat got turned around from Botany Bay last century.

Sure enough, the very next day Mark Waugh (complete with designer stubble which the politically correct toffs have banned among the England players) was lampooning the English lads, saying they had no fire in their bellies. Surely, doesn't the fact that they have to go into a management school with Will Carling speak volumes about what is wrong with English cricket?

My idea for toughening the lads up would be to get them on a jumbo jet and out to Hong Kong with 'Beefy' Botham and Gazza as tour leaders. They could then strap each other in a dentist's chair and discover some team spirit. This is what Terry Venables did and it didn't do too much harm for the England football boys. I don't want to alarm you, but Will Carling never won a big one against an Antipodean and his game plan with the wife fell apart when he sighted Lady Di.

Please don't confuse Pom with POMO. The former made Australia, while the latter confused a generation of football fans.

I await your reply.

William Egan

The Daily Mail
Northcliffe House, 2 Derry Street, Kensington, London W8 5TT

Mr William Egan
Guildford Road
Leatherhead
Surrey KT24 5NW

7 May 1997

Dear Bill,

Thank you for your very amusing letter. I can see you have grave reservations about Will Carling's motivational powers!

Best wishes,

Brian Scovell
Cricket Correspondent

Guildford Road
Leatherhead
Surrey KT24 5NW

Tony Blair
Prime Minister
10 Downing Street
London SW1A 2AA

4 May 1997

Dear Tony,

As Gary Glitter shouts every Christmas at his gang show: 'Leader, Leader!' Congratulations and magic! Are there enough superlatives in the English language to sum it all up? I doubt it, and as I am definitely not knowledgeable enough to know them all, I'll leave the written word to your trusted football writer, Sheffield Wednesday Roy. Now that you're in the new home you can look at which rooms the lads put up their football posters in.

Now, with the utmost respect, a word from your football advisor. It was football wot won it, so don't ditch football now that you've seen off John Boy. You've started well. The most important thing for a football team (and a government) is a strong spine. Firstly there's you in goal (I saw you in the publicity pictures in goal with Alex Ferguson, the unsmiling one from Manchester), and you have appointed an uncompromising centre-half in John 'nothing passes' Prescott. Your choice for centre-forward of Gordon Brown gives that strength down the middle. However, he is Scottish so I hope he has more self-control than that other well-known Scots centre-forward Duncan Disorderly of Everton. Robin Cook scheming at left midfield (all Europeans have left-sided tricky players; well done for seeing that) shows that you are in the know. As for the others, well, I hope that everybody has undergone their football knowledge test. Any man who forgets the power of football will soon find himself on the wrong side of the 'The Sun Says' crap leader writer. Not that you didn't know that, as you sorted out Uncle Rupert Murdoch long before the sun set on John Major.

Now, a quick word about policy. Manifestos cover all the pertinent points, but there is one point which needs addressing. Uncle Rupert and his Sky bods are scheduling football at increasingly strange times. It's not a problem, but some of the matches finish so late that after me and the chaps have left the stadium we barely have time for a swift half when someone shouts last orders at the bar. If I travel 20 miles across the channel this doesn't happen. Any

182

chance of you sorting out this law which, I believe, stems from the need for extra First World War ammunition? Correct me if I'm wrong, but didn't this fracas end a few years ago, or have my history books been misleading me? Football fans need to unwind after a hard day watching football, while some fans need to unwind more than others. Is it true that the House of Commons bar is open 24 hours a day when the chaps are in session? Now that is a session! Not even slaphead Willoughby Wellings can drink 24 hours a day.

It's good to see a man in power who really understands football, although I'll only truly believe it when I see you attending Highbury Stadium, the real home of football. I expect you are too busy at the moment with the nitty-gritty to address us yourself. No worries, mate, we understand. However, a word for the chaps would be appreciated.

Football's where it's at.

Pele played at No. 10 (so did Maradona, but don't get paranoid about that!).

William Egan

Copies to: Robin Cook, Foreign Secretary
            Gordon Brown, Chancellor of the Exchequer
            John Prescott, Deputy Prime Minster
            Claire Short, Heritage Minister
            Ken Livingstone, MP (once lefty bogey man of the Sun),
              Political Editor, the Guardian
            Peter Mandelson, Spin Bowler, Labour Party

10 Downing Street
London SW1A 2AA

From the Correspondence Secretary

Mr W. Egan
Guildford Road
Leatherhead
KT24 5NW

13 May 1997

Dear Mr Egan,

The Prime Minister has asked me to thank you for your recent letter, the terms of which have been carefully noted.

Mr Blair has asked that your letter be passed to the department with particular responsibility for the matter you raise so that they, too, are aware of your views.

Yours sincerely,

Frances Slee (Mrs)

Guildford Road
Leatherhead
Surrey KT24 5NW

John Major
Conservative Central Office
32 Smith Square
Westminster
London SW1P 3HH

4 May 1997

Dear John,

The curtain has fallen. Seeing you go was like watching Arsenal trudge off after we'd lost to Valencia on penalties in 1980. It took Arsenal 15 years to avenge that. Hope the omens aren't that bad.

I still think that you were outplayed with the footy card by Tony in midfield. Every picture saw him with the chaps kicking a ball, while your love was cricket. No disrespect, but football is on the up while cricket can just about raise itself out of the basement to send our chaps on self-improvement courses. I hope that you pass on the sound advice to your successor about getting in touch with the football ticket in order to get back in the ratings. At the moment the Conservatives are in the Vauxhall Conference, and it's a long way back into the Premier League.

I did write to all your policy bods telling them to play the football card, but they just ignored me. Bad move. While you were lobbing long European balls into the box, Tony was silkily passing the ball around in midfield. People like that fancy passing and pretty movement. Long ball and POMO are outdated. Look at the Premier League. Everybody is playing European, so your mob's disorganised ramblings about Europe being bad brought back the bad old days of long ball and Graham 'Turnip Head' Taylor.

In the words of Don Howe, who is a better defensive general than even Rommel, 'Politics is like a game of football. The team that makes the least number of mistakes will win the game.'

Enjoy your cricket, mate, but do me one last favour. Get in that dressing-room at Edgbaston before the first test against the Aussies and tell the lads to forget all that poofy rubbish, get out there and stuff it up 'em like real men!

William Egan

Copies to: David Mellor, ex-MP
               Seb Coe, ex-MP
               Mike Langley, sportswriter, Sunday Mirror

House of Commons
London SW1A 0AA

From the Office of the Leader of the Opposition

13 May 1997

Dear Mr Egan

Thank you for your letter to Mr Major of 4 May 1997. I have been asked to reply on his behalf.

It was kind of you to have taken the trouble to write as you did.

Letters such as yours are of great support and encouragement and Mr and Mrs Major are immensely grateful for all your kind words and good wishes.

Even though he is stepping down as leader of the party, Mr Major will of course continue to do everything he can to help a return to a Conservative government at the next general election.

The party must now unite, under a new leader, to secure such a victory and he will do all he can from the backbenches to bring it about.

Thank you for taking the trouble to write.

Yours sincerely,

Roderick Brown

Guildford Road
Leatherhead
Surrey KT24 5NW

Mike Langley
Sportswriter
The Sunday Mirror
Holborn Circus
London EC1P 1DQ

4 May 1997

Dear Mike,

As a man who never minces his words, apart from when you were summoned for a rollicking by Margaret Thatcher, I enclose a letter I have sent to John Major. He missed the boat big time because he didn't understand football!

Yours sincerely,

William Egan

Sunday Mirror

9 May 1997

Dear Mr Egan,

I was never rollicked by Mrs Thatcher or summoned to No. 10 for a reprimand in either of my visits. On the contrary, I made her laugh – 'more heartily than I've ever heard her,' said Bernard Ingham.

Also, Rommel was not primarily a defensive general; his reputation was founded on breathtaking attack in France 1941 and Libya in the following year.

Finally, I cannot support any plea to entice politicians into football. They should be kept at a safe distance from all sports.

Apart from these points, thanks for writing.

Mike Langley

Guildford Road
Leatherhead
Surrey KT24 5NW

Doug Ellis
Chairman
Aston Villa Football Club
Villa Park
Trinity Road
Birmingham B6 6HE

5 May 1997

Dear Doug,

I understand that your nickname is 'Deadly', due to your penchant for sacking managers. Nothing wrong with that; I'd sack managers every other week if I had plenty of money and nothing much else to do.

However, there is one burning question which I hope you can answer. Can you understand a word your current manager, Brian Little, says? He doesn't seem to talk the same language as other managers. No 'over the moon', 'boys done good' or 'sick as a parrot'; he's more of an expressed innovative movement man. Tell me, does he look at all that modern art stuff? If he does, it would explain the way he talks. Have you seen that tripe? It looks like someone has spilt paint on the canvas, and then reviewers talk about the expressionism coming from it.

Is this a ploy to confuse you? If you don't understand him, then how can you sack him? Whenever I see Villa on the TV and they interview Brian after the match, he seems confused. After he has finished speaking, so are the rest of us. If it is a tactic then it has most certainly paid off, because normally a Villa manager would get his cards after the mediocre season you've just had.

Imagine the conversations that must go on between that Yugoslavian Milosovic and Brian. The mind boggles.

William Egan

Aston Villa
Registered Office: Villa Park, Birmingham B6 6HE

Mr W. Egan
Guildford Road
Leatherhead
Surrey KT24 5NW

9 May 1997

Dear Mr Egan,

Thank you for your letter dated 5 May 1997 in which you question whether I can understand what Brian Little is talking about.

I can advise you quite categorically that I well understand his articulate and lucid explanations and I consistently receive congratulations from all quarters that we now have a manager at Villa Park who is able to express himself without using the tired old football clichés you refer to. Moreover, I can assure you that our players of all nationalities have absolutely no problem communicating with Brian Little.

Yours sincerely,

H.D. Ellis
Chairman

Guildford Road
Leatherhead
Surrey KT24 5NW

Howard Kendall
Manager
Sheffield United Football Club
Bramall Lane
Sheffield S2 4SU

5 May 1997

Dear Mr Kendall,

How is life in the steel city? You certainly are a man who believes in chasing lost causes: Manchester City, Notts County and now Sheffield United. Had you lived in another time I have no doubt you would have managed the Christians going into the Coliseum.

Being a man of the old school with a footballer's sense of humour, I can now see why you sold Nathan Blake. However, that is not why I am writing. We would like you to settle a bet between myself and the follically challenged 'Frenchy'.

You may know of the man in the Premier League called Jim Smith, Derby County's manager, whose sobriquet is the 'Bald Eagle'. Whilst watching a recent match on Sky TV, Strace the Ace stated to Frenchy that he was marginally less bald than Jim Smith but not as bald as Howard Kendall.

I consider that you have more hair than Jim Smith, but Strace reckoned he saw you at Crystal Palace this season and the grim reaper had really done a number on your hair. Being follically complete myself I reckon to be able to judge these matters better than those who are less fortunate up top. Notwithstanding the fact that I once read that bald men were more virile, this might be a touchy subject.

Please settle this bet, which almost got nasty, and confirm that you are indeed not the new Bald Eagle of Sheffield.

The Man of Steel for the Premiership!

William Egan

Sheffield United Football Club
Bramall Lane, Sheffield S2 4SU

Mr W. Egan
Guildford Road
Leatherhead
Surrey KT24 5NW

8 May 1997

Dear Mr Egan,

Many thanks for your recent letter.

Please don't insult me. I don't have the same hairstyle as Jim!

I hope this settles your bet!

Yours sincerely,

Howard Kendall
Manager

Guildford Road
Leatherhead
Surrey KT24 5NW

Jim Smith
Manager
Derby County Football Club
The Baseball Ground
Derby DE23 8NB

5 May 1997

Dear Mr Smith,

Good to see that the old touch of keeping clubs up hasn't deserted you. A man with your talents could have kept the *Titanic* up.

However, that is not the reason for writing. I believe you are called the 'Bald Eagle', due to your follically challenged appearance. I would like you to settle a bet between myself and fellow slaphead 'Frenchy'.

You may know of the man in the First Division called Howard Kendall, Sheffield United's manager, whose claim to fame is being sacked by Notts County for being drunk. Hell, I'd take to drink if I had to manage that bunch of underachievers after managing Everton to the success he did. Even Manchester City would seem like a champagne reception compared to that.

Whilst watching a recent match on Sky TV, Strace the Ace stated to Frenchy that he was even balder than the new Bald Eagle Howard Kendall. Someone in football balder than Jim Smith? I'm not having that.

If this is correct then you are no longer the 'Bald Eagle', and if Howard manages to get Sheffield up you will no longer have this unique sobriquet in the Premier Division. Strace reckoned he saw you at Chelsea this season and you looked like you'd had an Elton John down the sides of the bonce. This is a worrying trend: Jim Smith no longer the Bald Eagle? It's like Tommy Cooper without his fez. Notwithstanding the fact that I once read that bald men were more virile, this might be a touchy subject.

Please settle this bet, which almost got nasty, and confirm that you are still the undisputed Bald Eagle of the Football League.

Hair transplants are for wimps!

William Egan

SENT SIGNED PHOTOGRAPH

PS Any chance of a photo to settle the bet?

Guildford Road
Leatherhead
Surrey KT24 5NW

Jimmy Hill
Chairman
Fulham Football Club
Craven Cottage
London SW6 6HH

9 May 1997

Dear Jimmy,

What is happening, man? What happened to the Jimmy Hill of resolute thrusting chin, a man relied upon to give an opinion which people respected?

You are fast turning into a comedian. I don't care if you wish to do a turn on the stand-up circuit. (Trust me, you could do it. I've worked the door on some of those places and those guys just aren't funny. Every other word is eff this and eff that.) First you let that whinging jock Hansen blow you up, then you do a silly advert for scratchcards. Sort it, as Grant Mitchell says with frightening regularity on *Eastenders*.

No, me and the lads don't care what you are doing, it's just that we're worried about the effect you're having on Fulham Football Club. As long as you are seen as a music-hall turn then so will Fulham be. Look at Spurs. Alan Sugar goes on the TV last week to say that he won't rest until Spurs win the league. Mad Monty laughs so much we have to call an ambulance. It'll be like Rip Van Winkle in reverse; he'll never sleep. Now, every time we see an Amstrad we laugh.

I have been running a campaign to get Paddy Ashdown at the Fulham, because that man exudes trust and commitment. Together you can get back into the Premier League. I will have to stop it if everybody starts associating Fulham with a joke.

Get back to me on this, as I'm thinking of enrolling my lad, Alex James, into the junior Fulham club but can't even contemplate it if you're going through the menopause and think you're the next Paul Daniels (without the rug).

Fulham fans do it in the Cottage!

William Egan

194

Fulham Football Club
Craven Cottage, Stevenage Road, London SW6 6HH

27 May 97

Dear Bill,

You need have no worries now!

Yours sincerely,

Jimmy Hill
(Ex-Chairman)

Guildford Road
Leatherhead
Surrey KT24 5NW

Gerry Francis
Manager
Tottenham Hotspur Football Club
White Hart Lane
748 High Road
Tottenham
London N17 0AP

12 May 1997

Dear Gerry,

I am very worried about the man you work for, Alan Sugar. His paranoid outbursts are getting more frequent, especially now they have a gentleman Frenchman ensconced at the north London rivals and he's struggling for targets. Is he okay? I have been writing to him but he doesn't even answer his mail nowadays. Perhaps he's like Saddam Hussein, getting somebody to open his letters and then only reading the ones where people say something nice. (Mind you, whoever does that must only work five minutes per day – only joking!)

Anyway, watch him – he is starting to sound unstable. I also heard him say that you'd had a bet on Spurs to win something next season. Surely that isn't correct? I've heard you only spend your money on dead certs. You didn't shave your sideburns off and let your hair go grey to throw your money away on stupid bets.

Word is you also like the odd antique, but being linked to Old Jürgen Klinsmann, the wanderlust German, is a bit too far fetched. He's the only man I know who gets homesick when he's living in the country where he was born. A word of free advice: footballers don't gain in value when they get over 33; they tend to depreciate – rapidly.

Look at Spurs. Do you really need Jürgen to come back, only to lose in another FA Cup semi-final then get homesick again?

No. Buy English footballers.

William Egan

Tottenham Hotspur
748 High Road, Tottenham, London N17 0AP

Mr William Egan
Guildford Road
Leatherhead
Surrey KT24 5NW

18 June 1997

Dear Bill,

Sincere apologies for the delay in replying to your letter, but with the unusually large number of injuries our players sustained last season, the last few months have been very hectic indeed.

As I am sure you will appreciate, I have received thousands of letters from supporters. Some are from people with attitudes similar to yours, whilst some have a completely different opinion of the situation last season. Everyone is entitled to their own viewpoint, as indeed you are, but hopefully we all have the same aim behind our varying opinions – and that is to see this club successful and to bring some silverware to the Lane.

I, more than anyone else, know how frustrating it is to be in the same position each week with regard to the injuries, and I appreciate how frustrated you the fans must have felt week in week out when I gave you updates on the squad. But although we investigated our training methods and how the various injuries were sustained (approximately 90 per cent of the injuries were picked up in match situations), and although we obtained the best medical advice and treatment for the injured players, unfortunately there was nothing we could do to change 'lady luck'.

As with every club, our scouts are continuously looking for prospective players, but because of the unlucky run of injuries we have had, it has been important for us to double our efforts in our search for players to strengthen our squad. Last season we added Ramon Vega, Allan Nielsen, John Scales and Steffen Iversen to the squad. Ramon Vega and Allan Nielsen are current internationals and John Scales, who is also an international, has just been recalled into the England squad. Steffen Iversen is, I am sure you will agree, a great prospect at only 20 years of age. Unfortunately three of these four players had long-term injuries shortly after coming to the club, but should all be fit and well and ready for the new season.

197

As you know, a number of times last season we had to play with a relatively inexperienced side due to the injury crisis, and in fairness to the young pros such as Stephen Carr, Rory Allen, Neale Fenn, Espen Baardsen, Paul McVeigh, Jamie Clapham, etc. they did well and look encouraging prospects for the future. We had to field sides with up to 15 first-team players missing, and although every team gets injuries, we had all at once. When everybody is fit and well, I believe we have a very strong squad that, with a couple of additions this summer, can challenge and win some silverware in the coming season.

Hopefully myself and the players can count on your support because a club is not just made up of the manager and 11 players. It is much more than that. It is also made up of the whole squad, a large number of people who work behind the scenes and, most importantly, you the fans.

Thank you for your letter, and although you were not entirely happy with the team and the situation last season, hopefully we can rely on your continued support and reward your loyalty before too long by bringing some success to White Hart Lane.

With very best wishes.

Yours sincerely,

Gerry Francis
Manager

Guildford Road
Leatherhead
Surrey KT24 5NW

Steve Coppell
Manager
Crystal Palace Football Club
Selhurst Park
London SE25 6PU

14 May 1997

Dear Steve,

Few people in football realise that 1997 is the 25th anniversary of one of the great terrace battles: the yellow paint battle of the Shed. That day, a serious number of handpicked Arsenal and Chelsea chaps had a friendly battle and took along plenty of yellow paint, resulting in everybody going home with black eyes and yellow paint everywhere else.

To celebrate a real event, a few of the chaps are having an anniversary dinner at our local Italian nosherie. We are looking to bring in a celebrity guest speaker and would like to invite you to do the honours, so to speak.

Of course we'd pay you a fee, plus as many bread rolls as you can eat, and we could also arrange overnight accommodation upstairs at the Royal Oak. Don't worry, it's not haunted – although sometimes the landlord's wife has been mistaken for a ghost when she glides along the landing in her white chiffon nightie. Not that a man of your class would worry about such mundane things.

Don't panic if some of the lads look a little fierce, as Chits is going to put his best falsies in and Strace will wear a roll neck so that the 'cut here' tattoo on his neck doesn't show. The lads may once have been fearsome protagonists, but now they are all friendly family men who always dance the birdy song at weddings and regularly cheer when their lottery balls are drawn out.

Get back to me, as we're looking at doing this the first week of July.

Yours sincerely,

William Egan

Copies to: Graham Taylor, ex-England manager
              Jeff Powell, Chief Sportswriter, Daily Mail
              Brendan Batson, Deputy Chairman, PFA

Crystal Palace FC
Selhurst Park Stadium, London SE25 6PU

Mr William Egan
Guildford Road
Leatherhead
Surrey KT24 5NW

20 May 1997

Dear Mr Egan,

I am replying on Steve Coppell's behalf to your letter of 14 May 1997.

Before showing this to Steve I need to know the exact date for this evening of fun, as the team are due to start their pre-season tour on 8 July.

This doesn't mean that the answer will be yes, but at least I'll know if he can begin to consider it.

From my own point of view, the description of Chits and Strace means that it promises to be a night to remember!

Yours sincerely,

Clare Cunningham
Secretary to the Manager

Watford
Registered Office and Ground: Watford Association Football Club Ltd
Vicarage Road Stadium, Watford WD1 8ER

Mr W. Egan
Guildford Road
Leatherhead
Surrey KT24 5NW

22 May 1997

Dear Bill,

Thank you for your letter dated 14 May 1997.

In all seriousness, Bill, I am ready for a break and at the present time the last thing I need is accepting extra invitations, even though I know I would have a good time!

Please do not take offence by this reply, but I really have got to limit myself as to what I am taking on.

On 1 July we commence pre-season training and I think you will agree that is where my priority has to be – on the pitch and with the players again!

Best wishes,

Graham Taylor

The Daily Mail
Northcliffe House, 2 Derry Street, Kensington, London W8 5TT

Mr William Egan
Guildford Road
Leatherhead
Surrey KT24 5NW

22 May 1997

Dear Bill,

It was a pleasure to receive your amusing letter.

It would also have been a delight to speak at your dinner, but your timing is very difficult for me.

The end of June and the beginning of July are full up with things like the Tyson and Lewis fights, which will keep me in the US for the best part of three weeks between them. I also have to try to fit in Wimbledon and the Open.

There is also just the chance that I might get a week or two off at the end of July and beginning of August . . . which would make a change after last year, which had Euro 96 and the Atlanta Olympics on top of everything else.

Anyway, have a great dinner and I will drink a toast to you wherever I am at that time.

Thanks for thinking of me.

Yours sincerely,

Jeff Powell
Chief Sports Feature Writer

PS Tell the lads I may well see you in Poland. We'll be there!

Professional Footballers Association
2 Oxford Court, Bishopsgate, Manchester M2 3WQ

Mr W. Egan
Guildford Road
Leatherhead
Surrey KT24 5NW

30 May 1997

Dear Bill,

Thank you for your letter of 14 May and the invitation to be the guest speaker at your dinner.

Unfortunately I have a very busy diary at the start of July and thereafter I am away for the rest of July on my family holiday. I am therefore unable to accept your invitation.

Hope you have a good night.

Yours sincerely,

Brendan Batson
Deputy Chief Executive

Guildford Road
Leatherhead
Surrey KT24 5NW

John Prescott
Deputy Leader
Labour Party
150 Walworth Road
London SE17 1JJ

15 May 1997

Dear Fellow Seaman,

I have received no reply to my letter dated 8 March 1997. Don't worry, as I can see that you did finally take my advice on board (little bit of the naval flavour there, me old shipmate). About time, too, although I do feel that the delay may well have cost you 20 seats.

At least you eventually got Tony Blair on the TV kicking a ball around, which saw the ratings rise in the opinion polls. What's the difference between a three-card trickster and an opinion poll? Nothing. You can't trust either!

I've got back to Tony now the election's over to put in a good word. You're OK. I've read your autobiography and I like a man who lets it ride in the boozer when someone is dishing out the grief, then gives them a good slap the next morning while they've still got a hangover.

Lead with your left not your chin!

Pity I wasn't around last time to give the Taffy Kinnock some sound advice, or you'd be looking at a second term of office. As you're a real European now I enclose 10 deutschmarks for the return postage before it becomes an Emu, or whatever.

Up the reds.

William 'Right Cross' Egan

House of Commons
London SW1A 0AA

The Office of the Deputy Prime Minister

William 'Right Cross'(!) Egan
Guildford Road
Leatherhead
Surrey KT24 5NW

4 June 1997

Dear Fellow Seaman,

Thank you very much for your letter of 15 May.

I'm sorry if you received no reply from your earlier letter. I do try to make sure that all letters are answered but as you know we were pretty busy preparing for the election.

Things are even busier now but at least we are 'doing' rather than just 'saying'.

Thanks again for your comments.

Best wishes.

Yours sincerely,

Rt. Hon. John Prescott MP
Deputy Prime Minister

Guildford Road
Leatherhead
Surrey KT24 5NW

Ken Clarke MP
The House of Commons
London SW1A 0AA

28 May 1997

Dear Leadership Challenger,

Any man described in the Guardian as 'the bruiser's bruiser' gets the chaps' vote. Not that our votes will count in the final reckoning, but our advice will. The sound advice I gave to Tony Blair during the election campaign? Be seen kicking a football. He did just that. Result? Landslide.

Want to be the new leader of the Conservatives? Right, get on board with this. Football is big business and high profile at the current time, but I don't need to tell you that. Everybody is into football nowadays. Take Patsy Kensit, the blond bit with no boobs and obviously no taste, as she married that Liam Gallagher who is only slightly less belligerent than Tony Banks, Hon. Sports Minister. (Another Chelsea fan, and no doubt ex-Shed boy.) Now she is seen at Chelsea alongside all the other poseurs, she's being offered films that count.

Take a leaf out of her book. Get yourself along to the cup final. Shout anti-Europe slogans to get the Eurosceptics on your side and then shake hands with Ruud Gullit. Net result? Instant popularity ('That Clarkey man understands ECUs and egos'). Name me somebody popular today who isn't into football? Why did Thatcher get the chop? Because she didn't understand football, that's why. She once asked the sports press why football couldn't be played behind closed doors and then relayed to everybody's TV screen in their front room. (Mind you, the press boys didn't know the answer because, as usual, they'd spent too long in the bar.) Result? Thatcher booted out faster than you can say 'Labour landslide'.

The party leadership won't be won by fancy speeches on the TV shows of poncy commentators like Jeremy Paxman; it will be won because the bedraggled, defeated Tories perceive that the man at the helm can turn things around. As a European I enclose 20 French francs to help the war effort.

Get kicking (first the ball, then some butt)!

William Egan

House of Commons
London SW1A 0AA

Mr W. Egan
Guildford Road
Leatherhead
Surrey KT24 5NW

6 June 1997

Dear Mr Egan,

The Rt. Hon. Kenneth Clarke QC MP acknowledges with thanks the receipt of your communication of 28 May 1997, the contents of which have been noted.

House of Commons

Guildford Road
Leatherhead
Surrey KT24 5NW

Bill Campbell
Managing Director
Mainstream Publishing Co. (Edinburgh) Ltd
7 Albany Street
Edinburgh EH1 3UG

5 June 1997

Dear Bill,

Remember our conversation at L'Etoile restaurant last year when I was doing
the door for your bash for those rich and famous poofy writer types?

I told you about me writing to all those jumped-up poofs about the real issues
existing in football and life. Well, I have in my possession a large number of
letters from such famous people as Gary Lineker, Alex Ferguson, John
Prescott, the Prince of Wales and Nelson Mandela.

Would you like to see them? I believe it tells a unique story of the football
season which has just passed.

Yours sincerely,

William 'Bootsy' Egan